Y0-BVQ-708

Administrative Rulemaking

Administrative Rulemaking

POLITICS
AND PROCESSES

WILLIAM F. WEST

KF
5407
.W48
1985
WEST

CONTRIBUTIONS IN POLITICAL SCIENCE,
NUMBER 122

ASU WEST LIBRARY

GREENWOOD PRESS
Westport, Connecticut
London, England

Library of Congress Cataloging in Publication Data

West, William F.
   Administrative rulemaking.

   (Contributions in political science, ISSN 0147-1066 ;
no. 122)
   Includes bibliographical references and index.
   1. Administrative procedure—United States.   I. Title.
II. Title: Administrative rule-making.   III. Series.
KF5407.W48   1985   342.73′066   84-12825
ISBN 0-313-24157-0 (lib. bdg.)   347.30266

Copyright © 1985 by William F. West

All rights reserved. No portion of this book may be
reproduced, by any process or technique, without the
express written consent of the publisher.

Library of Congress Catalog Card Number: 84-12825
ISBN: 0-313-24157-0
ISSN: 0147-1066

First published in 1985

Greenwood Press
A division of Congressional Information Service, Inc.
88 Post Road West
Westport, Connecticut 06881

Printed in the United States of America

10 9 8 7 6 5 4 3 2 1

For my mother, Constance West

● *Contents*

• *Illustrations*

FIGURE

TABLES

● *Acknowledgments*

I am grateful to the present and former FTC officials, congressional staffers, and others in Washington who were so generous with their time in answering my questions. Jon Bond, Bonnie Browne, Dwight Davis, George Greanias, Mike Levy, Roby Robertson, Elizabeth Sanders, Harvey Tucker, and Chuck Wiggins have read various parts of this manuscript or related works, and all have offered sound criticism and advice. Special thanks in this regard go to my mentor and friend Joe Cooper. Terry Schiefen has been extremely competent and patient in typing and revising my manuscript, and Jackie Ehlers has helped me in ways too numerous to mention.

Administrative Rulemaking

●1 Introduction

The administrative process has an important role in the American political system. Administrative forms and procedures serve as means through which we attempt to legitimate, or at least live with, delegations of policy-making authority to non-elected officials. As a substitute for detailed substantive guidance, which often proves impossible or impractical, we structure the exercise of bureaucratic discretion to ensure that it conforms as far as possible with our beliefs and values concerning how agency decisions should be made. The administrative process is also important because the rules of the game are seldom neutral in their impact on the various interests who stand to be affected by agency decisions.

It is unfortunate that political scientists have shown so little interest in formal rules, structures, and procedures in recent decades. Although the abandonment of "legalistic description" as the sole focus of the discipline has been well founded, the consideration of institutions can be integrated with the consideration of political behavior to gain a better understanding of how policy is made. Such an approach has prescriptive as well as heuristic value. Institutional analysis is especially appropriate in the area of public administration given the great expansion of delegated authority that has occurred over the past twenty years, coupled with the proliferation of mechanisms designed to structure agency discretion. In this regard, the element of the administrative process which is perhaps most worthy of attention is rulemaking.

THE NEED FOR INSTITUTIONAL POLICY ANALYSIS

As Vincent Ostrom observes, constitutional analysis has become a forgotten tradition.[1] Whereas the primary focus of political science was once upon the normative bases for and the practical implications of formal institutional arrangements, such considerations have, in large part, been abandoned as irrelevant. This fundamental change in orientation may have had its origins in the late 1800s and early 1900s, as Ostrom argues. Certainly, disillusionment with formal structure as an explanation for political phenomena was evident in the works of several leading scholars of the era, such as Frank Goodnow and Charles Beard.[2] It was perhaps most explicit in the writing of Woodrow Wilson, who, for example, argued in 1885 that the American political system had become one of congressional government, and that the constitutional balance of powers devised by the founding fathers had become merely a "facade."[3] Of course, attention to structure did not cease abruptly. Institutional analysis and design remained an important element of the discipline well into the 1930s, especially in the area of public administration. By mid-century, however, political science had become predominantly a "value free endeavor to determine who exercises power," in which form was considered to be of "little or no significance."[4]

Institutional scholarship of the past was often narrow and descriptive, ignoring the effects of important social and economic variables. The great virtue of behaviorism is that it has focused our attention on these "informal" determinants of politics. Even though institutional considerations fail to provide a sufficient explanation for government action, however, it is fallacious to assume that they are unimportant. While few, of course, would subscribe to such an extreme view, the notion that formal structure can be ignored has served as at least an operational assumption behind most of the research on American politics in recent decades. This perspective has impaired analysis, for institutions typically interact with other factors to affect the political process in important ways, both intended and unintended. In this sense, rules and structures often channel, shape, and determine the relative magnitude of various non-institutional forces, such as group pressure and public opinion.

Institutional analysis which integrates formal structure with informal considerations can thus make important contributions to our knowledge about the political process. It can also be used in designing institutions which are appropriate in light of the expectations we hold for government. Several sorts of considerations provide the basis for such an approach. As Ostrom states:

At the constitutional level of analysis, one is concerned with basic questions of why human beings have recourse to political institutions, and what options are available. One is also concerned about what implications follow from alternative possibilities and what criteria are used, or what purposes are served, in the choices that are made among alternative possibilities. Thus, political theory has a special relevance for the constitutional level of analysis. The constitutional level of analysis has a fundamental role in clarifying the design of structural arrangements that apply to the play of the game of politics. The play of a game is determined by the rules of the game; and the rules establishing the terms and conditions of governance are constitutional in character. The constitutional level of analysis, then, informs the operational level of analysis of who gets what, when, and how.[5]

Analysis should be concerned in part, then, with explanation. Political theory is important here, as Ostrom notes. Notwithstanding the cynicism of many students of politics, institutions are typically based upon widely shared normative principles. At the same time, however, abstract considerations of good government are seldom adequate explanations in themselves. Those who stand to be affected by what government does typically perceive that some institutional arrangements are more conducive to their interests than others, and they exert influence upon the choice among alternative rules and structures accordingly.

Analysis should also be concerned with the effects of institutions. Perhaps the most important criterion to be used here is whether rules and structures actually promote the normative goals or group interests they were intended to serve. Relatedly, it is important to consider unintended or side effects. Although a given device may further its intended objectives in one way, it may detract from the same or other goals in another. And finally, it is useful to examine consistency both within and among institutional arrangements. Different mechanisms, or aspects of mechanisms, may promote common or reinforcing objectives, or they may work at cross-purposes.

The analysis of underlying rationale and the analysis of effects complement one another. The former enables us to identify the values our policy makers hope to promote through their choice of institutions; the latter tells us whether those values are, in fact, served, as well as whether other values are affected, either positively or negatively. Such an empirical approach to institutional analysis, in which considerations of intent and effect are integrated, has obvious prescriptive value in terms of intelligent institutional design. It is also a task for which political scientists are especially well suited.[6]

THE ANALYSIS OF ADMINISTRATIVE INSTITUTIONS

These basic perspectives can be applied fruitfully in the analysis of administrative institutions. As Colin Diver states, "Administrative law is, in essence, a search for a theory of how public policy should be made."[7] From a broad, constitutional perspective, therefore, structural arrangements and procedural requirements, which are designed to ensure desired, abstract qualities in the implementation of statutes, reflect particular sets of normative and practical assumptions concerning the sorts of decisional criteria agencies should take into account, as well as the processes appropriate for weighing alternative courses of action in light of those criteria. Given this, it is useful to ask whether the models which provide the bases for administrative institutions jibe with reality. Structural devices which are based on faulty premises or which reflect conflicting assumptions can (and do) impair the ability of agencies to carry out their mandates effectively.

In a narrower, political sense, administrative procedures and structures also "tend to favor some interests in society over others, some policy results rather than others."[8] One way they do this is by determining who can participate effectively in the administrative process, either through legal strictures or practical constraints. In a similar fashion administrative institutions can affect participation and the substance of policy by defining what is and what is not appropriate decisional input. Potentially affected interests are usually aware of these strategic implications of structural devices and attempt to influence the choice of administrative institutions accordingly (although their arguments are typically couched in terms of the public interest, constitutional principles, and the like). The struggle over administrative procedures is sometimes as intense as the struggle over substantive policy, and institutional arrangements are often the product of accommodation among competing interests.

Recent developments in the administrative process have increased the salience of institutional analysis. As delegated regulatory authority has grown so dramatically since the mid–1960s, so have efforts by Congress, the courts, and the executive to structure agency discretion. These efforts have been motivated in part by a desire to mitigate the increasing tension created for our political system by bureaucratic policy making, and have also come at the behest of groups who have perceived correctly that their stake in the administrative process has grown. The impact of institutional developments in regulatory administration over the past twenty years has likely been substantial in a number of respects. Available evidence suggests that structural and procedural changes have often been a source of differential advantage, for example. In addition, institutional arrangements have sometimes been based upon erroneous assumptions concerning the nature of agency decision making and have limited the effectiveness and even the integrity of the administrative process as a result.

It would be wrong to convey the impression that the sorts of concerns described here have been ignored. While political sci-

entists have devoted little attention to administrative institutions, a number of legal scholars have done some excellent
work in the area of late. Among others, Richard Stewart, James
Freedman, Kenneth Davis, Colin Diver, Barry Boyer and Martin Shapiro (a political scientist turned law professor) have
made important contributions to our understanding of the role
of administrative procedures in American politics. Still, such
matters have received relatively little attention and often have
been subordinate to legal questions where they have been
considered.

   This book focuses upon the use of administrative rulemaking
as a means of carrying out statutes, and upon requirements
used to guide and delimit rulemaking decisions. The primary
aim is to assess the ways in which these structural mechanisms
fit into the policy-making process. Thus, emphasis is placed on
the political determinants and effects of procedural choice. Of
course, rulemaking is only one of many elements in the administrative process. As quasi-legislation, however, it is the
most visible and direct means of bureaucratic policy making,
and in some ways the most troublesome for our political system.
   Furthermore, recent developments have increased the im--
portance of rulemaking as an area of inquiry. First, the use of
rulemaking has become much more pervasive throughout the
federal regulatory bureaucracy. Whereas students of administration formerly decried the failure of agencies to issue rules,
the 1970s have been referred to as the era of rulemaking. In
addition, several types of procedural and oversight requirements have become common as means of controlling rulemaking decisions. Though the use of rulemaking has often been
required or encouraged in recent years as a means of promoting
desired qualities in the administrative process it has also led
to more precipitous agency policy making and has therefore
exacerbated the tension inherent under broad mandates. Congress, the courts, and the executive have emphasized various
structural devices as means of ensuring that rules fall within
acceptable bounds as the result.
   The growth of administrative policy making has created a
great deal of tension for our political system. Broad delegations

of discretionary authority have been sanctioned by the courts and have increased dramatically in the interest of governmental effectiveness. Yet they have also been perceived as violations of our basic governmental principles and as being undesirable in a variety of other ways as well. As mentioned, administrative forms and procedures can be viewed in part as efforts to mitigate the problems presented by delegated authority. Not surprisingly, then, structural devices typically reflect long-standing norms concerning bureaucracy and its proper role in government, together with our disillusionment concerning unconstrained bureaucratic discretion. Chapter 2 provides a brief overview of the growth of delegated authority and the problems this development has presented for American democracy.

The third chapter defines administrative rulemaking and examines its use and its significance as a means of carrying out regulatory mandates. Although there has been some debate as to its merits, rulemaking has been widely advocated over the years. Perhaps most importantly, it is felt that rules promote formal justice, or the rule of law through the establishment of prospective standards for conduct, limiting arbitrariness, capriciousness, and retroactivity as policies are being applied in individual cases. Rulemaking is also felt to be a more forceful, comprehensive, and rational approach to policy making than adjudication, under which standards tend to be based on limited information and tend to be developed in an *ad hoc*, incremental fashion, if at all. Given the advantages claimed for rulemaking, administrators were frequently criticized in the past for their tendency to proceed in a rudderless, adjudicatory fashion. In recent years, however, agencies have relied heavily on rulemaking, partly as the result of their own initiative and partly as the result of requirements or prodding by Congress and the courts.

Chapter 4 is concerned with means of structuring rulemaking decisions. If rulemaking is perceived to be advantageous in important respects, it is also the most forceful and precipitous way in which agencies make policy. Not surprisingly, therefore, the expanded use of rulemaking in recent years has been accompanied by a variety of structural devices supplementing the Administrative Procedure Act's (APA's) simple notice-and-comment provisions (which place few constraints on agency discretion). Among the most important developments in this regard have been the extension of due process requirements to rulemaking, the stipulation that agencies use cost-benefit analysis to evaluate proposed regulations, and, otherwise, the expansion of opportunities for affected interests to participate in and influence agency decision making. In addition, Congress, the courts, and the executive have each attempted to improve their rulemaking oversight capabilities through institutional means.

The next two chapters present a case study examining the political and normative determinants as well as the policy effects of rulemaking and rulemaking procedure in the Federal Trade Commission (FTC). As discussed in Chapter 5, the FTC began issuing Trade Regulation Rules (TRRs) to "prevent unfair or deceptive practices" in 1961. Until that time it had relied on adjudication as its only formal consumer protection tool. Despite the various advantages claimed for rulemaking in terms of good administration, political considerations ultimately induced the FTC's changed approach. Rulemaking was strongly encouraged by those critical of the Commission's alleged passiveness and was adopted as a more forceful means of regulation as the consumer movement gained strength.

The Commission's early efforts were hindered by the fact that it lacked explicit statutory authority to issue rules. In response to this problem, a pro-consumer legislature passed the Magnuson-Moss Act in 1974, allaying all controversy concerning the legality of TRRs. In addition, however, Congress included procedures in the act considerably more stringent than the Administrative Procedure Act's simple notice-and-comment requirements (which had constrained FTC rulemaking up until that point). These procedures provided opportunities for interested parties to cross-examine and rebut in FTC hearings and required that the agency base its final decisions on the "substantial evidence" contained in a record. It also authorized funds to aid affected interests who lacked the resources necessary to participate effectively in FTC rulemaking.

Magnuson-Moss procedures stemmed partly from a desire to

confine rulemaking discretion within acceptable bounds. Congressmen—even liberal ones—were ambivalent about such a broad delegation of legislative authority and endeavored to ensure through institutional means that FTC rules would be well reasoned, that they would be based on legislative intent, and that they would reflect the input of relevant social interests. "Judicialized" procedures were also a concession to business groups, who perceived that such provisions would prove to be advantageous as a means of delaying and discouraging the issuance of TRRs.

As discussed in Chapter 6, the FTC responded to the Magnuson-Moss Act's apparent encouragement of aggressive regulation by proposing a series of ambitious TRRs in the mid–1970s. Somewhat ironically, however, very few of the Commission's rulemaking proceedings have come to fruition, even though most have been in progress for seven years or more. The FTC's failure to promulgate TRRs has been due in large part to the political repercussions of its rulemaking. As a more comprehensive and precipitous means of formulating policy, rulemaking has helped bring about an unprecedented reaction against the Commission from the business community and ultimately from Congress.

The FTC's difficulties in rulemaking can also be attributed in part to the procedures imposed by Magnuson-Moss. In practice, these requirements have helped ensure the viability of public participation in some respects. They have also helped ensure that TRRs are based on sound factual and legal premises. At the same time, however, Magnuson-Moss requirements have contributed to delay and deadlock in rulemaking proceedings, largely because they have been inappropriate for dealing with the sorts of broad policy issues raised by proposed TRRs. Judicialized procedures have made it difficult for the Commission to rely on its own expertise or to seek accommodation among competing interests, and have thus exacerbated the political difficulties inherent in rulemaking itself.

The final chapter takes a broad look at the reasons for and implications of recent developments in the administrative process, drawing on the FTC's experience and other available evidence. Efforts to structure bureaucratic discretion have, in large part, been informed by one or both of two fundamental values: rationality and responsiveness. While each of these goals has a long history as a guiding principle for public administration, each is based on a very different set of assumptions concerning the nature of agency decision making. The desire for rationality reflects the assumption that agency decision making is, or can be, a technocratic pursuit of predefined goals. On the other hand, the desire for responsiveness reflects the assumption that goals have not been defined by the legislature—at least not completely—and that agency decision making should therefore be based on the consideration of relevant social interests.

The net result of efforts to promote both rationality and responsiveness in the exercise of bureaucratic discretion has been to promote interest representation, but within the context of procedures which require means-end analyses of agency actions. This has likely impaired the administrative process in important ways. Agencies have been rendered less efficient as they have struggled to provide rational justifications for policies which are based in part on value premises, or on disputed factual or legal assertions. Opponents of regulation have been able to contribute to administrative delay by challenging the analyses which accompany proposed actions. The bases of administrative policy making have also become less straightforward as it has become necessary for agencies and participants in their proceedings to disguise policy preferences as legal and technical arguments. This, in turn, has undermined broad-based accountability in the administrative process. It has also imposed a bias in favor of those groups possessing the resources necessary for effective participation.

NOTES

1. Vincent Ostrom, "A Forgotten Tradition: The Constitutional Level of Analysis," in Judith A. Gillespie and Dina A. Zinnes, eds., *Missing Elements in Political Inquiry* (Beverly Hills: Sage Publications, 1982).

2. Frank Goodnow, *Politics and Administration: A Study in Government* (New York: Macmillan, 1900); Charles Beard, *An Economic Interpretation of the Constitution of the United States* (New York: Free Press, 1965). Cited in Ostrom, *supra* note 1, pp. 245–49.

3. Woodrow Wilson, *Congressional Government* (New York: Meridian, 1885), p. 28. Quoted in Ostrom, *supra* note 1, p. 246.

4. *Ibid.*, p. 249.

5. *Ibid.*, p. 237.

6. *Ibid.*, p. 250.

7. Colin S. Diver, "Policymaking Paradigms in Administrative Law," *Harvard Law Review*, 95 (December, 1981) p. 393.

8. James Anderson, *Public Policy-Making* (New York: Praeger Publishers, 1975) p. 24.

•2 The Dilemma of Administrative Discretion

We have strong misgivings about administrative discretion for a variety of reasons. Most importantly, perhaps, it seems to violate fundamental tenets of our constitutional democracy. Also, discretion is felt to be a source of (or at least a precondition for) arbitrary or unreasonable government behavior, and a leading cause of policy failure as statutes are being implemented. Yet despite these problems, the delegation of authority to administrative officials has continued to expand and indeed has accelerated rapidly in recent years. The resulting tension constitutes a fundamental dilemma for American government. This is especially true in the area of regulation, where agency discretion is typically broad, and where decisions often affect rights and duties and have significant economic impact.

As a prelude to the subsequent examination of attempts to structure agency decision making, this chapter provides an overview of administrative discretion, its growth, and the problems it presents. Included is a brief discussion of judicial precedent concerning the constitutionality of delegated authority. Kenneth Culp Davis' general definition of discretion as the "freedom to make a choice among possible courses of action or inaction" will suffice for the present, although at a later point it will be useful to distinguish types or elements of discretion.[1]

THE EXPANSION OF ADMINISTRATIVE DISCRETION

Agencies and the president have been vested with significant discretionary powers since the first days of the Republic. For example, the first session of Congress authorized the head of each department to "prescribe rules and regulations not inconsistent with the law, for the government of his Department, the conduct of its officers, the distribution of its business, and the custody, use, and preservation of the records, papers, and property appertaining thereto."[2] Also, the chief executive and other administrative officials were authorized to issue regulations to achieve a variety of generally stated policy goals. The president, for instance, was given the power to regulate all trade with the Indians, and the secretary of the treasury was given discretion to "regulate ... the marks to be set upon casks of distilled spirits and the forms of the certificates which are to accompany the same."[3]

Delegated authority has always existed; however, both its nature and its magnitude have evolved dramatically. In his 1927 study of federal legislation, John Comer divides the "history of national lawmaking" into four periods—1789–1824, 1825–1860, 1861–1890, and 1891–1926. He offers the following statements as a summary of his findings:

the legislature was inclined to share the burden of legislation with the executive often during the first period;... this practice was continued to some extent during the second;... Congress was liberal in delegating discretion during the third period; and ... during the fourth period the practice was generally established. Furthermore, although the President received a major portion of all delegated legislation during the first three periods, a division of labor was appearing in the administrative branch of the government and the basis for practically all legislative powers exercised at the present time by the major departments was being laid.[4]

Comer was prescient in implying that although delegated authority had always been significant, its exercise by agencies (as opposed to the president) would burgeon in the future.

Many have noted that bureaucratic policy making was quite

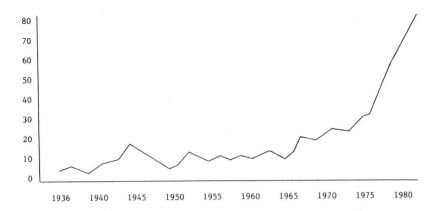

Figure 2.1
Growth of Federal Register (in thousands of pages)

limited in scope prior to the New Deal. James Wilson, for instance, states that "during its first 150 years, the American Republic was not thought to have a 'bureaucracy,' and thus it would have been meaningless to refer to the 'problems' of a 'bureaucratic state.' "[5] Since the 1930s, however, a tremendous expansion of the scope of federal activity has been accompanied by a like increase in the size of bureaucracy and in administrative output. The *Federal Register*, which is a daily publication of new agency rules, orders, and other actions, is often cited as a crude illustration of this latter development. The *Register* totaled 2,619 pages in 1936, the first year that it was published. After more than forty years of continued increase, the 1980 volume totaled in excess of 87,000 pages. As Figure 2.1 suggests, the rate of activity by federal agencies has increased dramatically in recent years.

An important share of the growth in bureaucratic policy making has occurred in the area of regulation. Since the mid–1960s, a number of new agencies have been created to regulate energy production and conservation, environmental quality, consumer products, and safety, among other things. Among the most important of these are the Equal Employment Opportunity Commission (EEOC), the Environmental Protection Agency (EPA), the Occupational Safety and Health Administration (OSHA), the Consumer Product Safety Commission (CPSC), the Nuclear Regulatory Commission (NRC), and the National Highway Traffic Safety Administration (NHTSA). While definitions of "regulation" vary considerably, according to Murray Weidenbaum the total number of federal regulatory agencies increased from twenty-nine in 1960 to fifty-five in 1979.[6] Beyond the creation of new agencies, Congress has also extended significantly the responsibilities of many existing regulatory bodies.

All told, Weidenbaum counts forty-two major pieces of regulatory legislation enacted between 1962 and 1979.[7] Many of these statutes have expressed very general goals conferring broad policy-making discretion upon agencies. For instance, the National Traffic and Motor Vehicle Safety Act, the Consumer Product Safety Act, and the Occupational Safety and Health Act instruct administrators to prevent "unreasonable risks" in many contexts. Also, recent statutes have often given agencies the authority to regulate, not one industry (as was the case under most older regulatory mandates), but a broad spectrum of commercial activities. The mandates given to OSHA, EPA, CPSC, and EEOC, for example, give those agencies power to monitor and control particular categories of behavior in all or most industries.

Several explanations have been offered for the growth of administrative discretion. One that has become popular among political scientists of late is that general mandates serve congressional interests. David Mayhew and Morris Fiorina argue in this regard that vague mandates enhance opportunities for congressmen to build constituent support through casework, and hypothesize that the expansion of the bureaucratic state largely explains the increased advantage incumbents have come to enjoy at the polls in recent years.[8] Another notion that has gained some currency is that committee or subcommittee members profit from vague legislation which allows policy to be

warped during implementation in such a way as to serve the narrow, complementary interests of subsystem actors.[9]
Notwithstanding such conspiracy theories, the growth of delegated authority is most often and most plausibly explained as a response to twentieth-century needs for government action. Elihu Root realized the inevitability of extensive administrative policy making as early as 1916, when he stated:

We are entering upon the creation of a body of administrative law quite different in its machinery, its remedies, and its necessary safeguards from the old methods of regulation by specific statutes enforced by the courts.... The necessities of our situation have already led to an extensive employment of that method.... Before these agencies the old doctrine prohibiting the delegation of legislative power has virtually given up the fight. There will be no withdrawal from these experiments. We shall go on; we shall expand them, whether we approve theoretically or not, because such agencies furnish protection to rights and obstacles to wrongdoing which under our new social and industrial conditions cannot be practically accomplished by the old and simple procedures of legislation and courts as in the last generation.[10]

As Root predicted, continued social, economic, and technological developments have spawned demands for regulation in a broad range of policy areas. The formulation and expression of such demands has been aided by increases in the levels of citizen education and awareness, and relatedly, by tremendous advances in the communications field. As Congress has responded by creating new programs, there has been a concomitant growth in delegated authority for several reasons.
Most obviously, the legislature has simply had to spread limited institutional resources among more areas as its workload has increased. This has left less time for mastering the substantive details of individual policies. Equally as important is the fact that the expanded scope of legislative activity has left less time for majority building in individual cases, thus increasing the imperative for Congress to settle for consensus on general rather than specific statutory goals. To be sure, legislative staff has been enlarged considerably in an attempt

to mitigate these problems, but its growth has lagged far behind increasing policy demands.

The need for flexibility in the effective pursuit of legislative goals has also increased the attractiveness of vague directives. Some have suggested, for example, that the mandate of the National Labor Relations Board (NLRB) to ensure "good faith bargaining" may not lend itself to further refinement as an abstract principle; rather, its meaning may have to be determined by the agency largely within the context of particular cases.[11] Discretion also serves the need for flexibility in coping with changes over time in technology, social conditions, or other factors relevant to an agency's mission. As an illustration, a statute enumerating all of items which the Consumer Products Safety Commission could regulate would leave the agency unable to confront safety hazards posed by new products.

Finally, Congress may delegate broad policy-making authority because it lacks knowledge about the problem it is attempting to confront. With advancing technology, this has become increasingly important as an explanation for regulatory discretion. Sometimes knowledge is not available because the problem is new, as when the Federal Communications Commission (FCC) was established to regulate a nascent broadcast industry in the "public interest, convenience, or necessity."[12] Alternatively, relevant knowledge may exist, but may not reside in the legislature. Congress may articulate general goals in such instances with the expectation that administrative experts will fill in the policy details. In fact, this has occurred often. Since the New Deal, the notion that bureaucratic expertise will provide efficient solutions to problems has often served as a justification for expansive delegations. To quote James Landis, a leading "New Deal intellectual,"

with the rise of regulation the need for expertness became dominant: for the art of regulating an industry requires knowledge of the details of its operation, ability to shift requirements as the conditions of the industry may dictate, the pursuit of energetic measures upon the appearance of an emergency, and the power through enforcement to realize conclusions as to policy.[13]

DISCRETION AND THE CONSTITUTION

However violative of strict constitutional interpretations, the courts have accommodated the growth of administrative discretion in regulatory areas and elsewhere. The U. S. Constitution does not deal specifically with the issue of delegated authority. Some have suggested that due to the limited scope of government at the time, the founding fathers did not anticipate the need to confer large grants of authority upon administrative officials. Be this as it may (again, there have been substantial delegations since the First Congress), the vagueness of the Constitution has precipated a long debate over the legal limits of administrative discretion. As in other matters, however, issues of constitutional theory have given way to the practical needs of modern government.

Several legal arguments have been offered against broad delegations of authority to administrative officials. Perhaps the most important of these revolve around the prescription of Article 1, Section 1, that "all Legislative Powers herein granted shall be vested in a Congress of the United States, which shall consist of a Senate and a House of Representatives." Many have contended that this language requires that policy be made by elected representatives, and that delegation therefore violates the Constitution's *specification of powers*. This is especially the case where agencies exercise discretion through the quasi-legislative process of rulemaking. An equally important argument has been that delegation violates *separation of powers*, since regulatory agencies operating under broad mandates typically possess substantial authority to legislate, execute, and adjudicate.[14]

Other legal arguments have been made against delegation as well. One is the common law maxim that power which is originally delegated cannot be redelegated. Another rests on the concept of due process. The reasoning here has been that clear legislative standards are a prerequisite for effective judicial review, since the courts have no basis for determining whether agencies have applied the law fairly to individuals in the absence of statutory guidance. As Robert Cushman states:

"To permit . . . an agency to exercise legislative power without the restraining influences of legislative 'standards' is to subject the citizen to the danger of an arbitrary power against which he may have no very effective protection."[15]

Defenses of delegation have also come in a variety of forms. For example, Kenneth Davis contends that the "necessary and proper" clause of Article 1, Section 8, implicitly bestows upon Congress the ability to delegate authority. He argues by way of analogy that the Constitution's stipulation that Congress collect taxes and coin money was certainly no indication that the framers expected the legislature actually to execute these tasks.[16] In another liberal interpretation of the separation of powers doctrine, John Cheadle argues that "sub-delegation," *per se*, is not unconstitutional so long as it is done pursuant to general guidelines. The constraints on Congress are minimal in his view, for he feels Section 8 of Article 1 is only "a prohibition of the attempted subdelegation of . . . the duty of meeting in annual session and declaring the national will in some form of enactment in the general laws."[17]

Scholars have also attempted to justify administrative discretion on the basis of historical evidence. Perhaps the most convincing argument along these lines is made by James Hart. He notes that many of the members of the Constitutional Convention and of the state ratifying conventions—men who presumably knew the true intent of the Constitution—subsequently held key positions in the three branches of government. Since Congress saw fit to confer, and administrative officials to carry out, broad, quasi-legislative powers from the very first, it is logical to assume that delegation did not violate the framers' intent. Hart supports this argument with the observation that at least three early Supreme Court decisions confirmed that the powers of the executive included quasi-legislation.[18]

Of course, the judiciary has borne ultimate responsibility for dealing with the controversial issue of delegation. Although the courts have been inconsistent on this question, both in regard to the legality and allowable limits of administrative discretion, most scholars seem to agree that decisions have followed a general historical pattern. The conservative courts of the late 1800s and early 1900s expressed the view that the delegation of legislative authority by Congress was unconstitutional. An important qualification, however, is that only two decisions—both rendered in 1935—actually declared specific delegations unconstitutional.[19] Aside from these anomalous cases, courts of the "non-delegation era" typically groped for ways to rationalize their decisions upholding particular delegations. For instance, the Supreme Court's 1892 *Field v. Clark* decision, which upheld a broad grant of rulemaking authority to the president, included the following justification:

> The legislature cannot delegate its power to make a law; but it can make a law to delegate a power to determine some fact or state of things upon which the law makes, or intends to make, its action depend. To deny this would be to stop the wheels of government. There are many things upon which wise and useful legislation must depend which cannot be known to the law making power and must, therefore, be a subject of inquiry outside the halls of legislation.[20]

In other instances, the courts attempted to resolve the conflict between their decisions and the non-delegation doctrine by implying that delegated authority was somehow not legislative in nature, provided that it was delimited by clearly articulated congressional directives. Thus, as Davis states, "The verbiage gradually developed that a delegation was lawful only when accompanied by a sufficient standard." In his analysis, the "sufficient standard" concept provided the transition out of the non-delegation era.[21]

The non-delegation doctrine has long since passed by the way. Some scholars and jurists still cling to the notion that delegated authority must be accompanied by a sufficient standard, but what constitutes such a standard is no more clear today than it was in Chief Justice Marshall's time.[22] Again to speak in practical terms, the first and last two instances in which delegations were declared *ultra vires* occurred in 1935. Since then, exceedingly broad policy-making mandates have gone untouched by the courts.

The issue of the constitutionality of delegated authority has never been resolved by the courts; it has just become mute. The judiciary's willingness to accept delegated legislative authority in practically any form has clearly been a response to felt policy needs rather than to purely legal considerations. As Ernst Freund put it some time ago, the justification for delegation is "one of convenience, primarily to relieve the legislature of a mass of detail, secondarily perhaps to gain greater flexibility."[23] The *Sunshine Anthracite* opinion, which states that delegation is necessary in order that the "expression of legislative power does not become a futility," summarizes the rationale of the courts most succinctly.[24]

THE PROBLEMS POSED BY DELEGATED AUTHORITY FOR AMERICAN GOVERNMENT

Although delegated authority has been sanctioned and has grown in the interest of expediency, it also creates important problems for our political system. Attitudes concerning the propriety and allowable limits of bureaucratic discretion cover a wide spectrum, but few would disagree that broad agency policy making violates fundamental American norms concerning institutional responsibilities and beliefs about institutional competency. The perceived illegitimacy of administrative discretion has been reinforced by a good deal of empirical evidence which suggests that broad delegations adversely affect the policy implementation process in a variety of ways.

Notwithstanding the court's abandonment of the non-delegation doctrine, many Americans find it difficult to reconcile bureaucratic policy making with fundamental democratic constitutional principles. The purpose of an elected legislature is to promote broad representation, citizen access, and responsiveness as policy decisions are being made, as well as accountability after the fact. There are, of course, no mechanisms to ensure these qualities in the administrative process—at least in a direct sense. The traditional justification that the exercise of delegated authority merely serves to fill up the details of legislation has remained patently unconvincing. This has especially been true in the area of regulation, where general mandates have often provided very little policy guidance.

Delegated authority is also perceived as violating the constitutional principle of limited power. As mentioned, agencies operating under broad mandates must often perform significant legislative, as well as executive and judicial, functions, and many fear that this creates the potential for excessive or arbitrary action. One authority notes:

> There can be little question that the theory of separation of powers ... retains an enduring hold on the American imagination. It has come to function as something of an idealized archetype, bequeathed to present generations by farsighted realists of past generations.... The administratve process does not, of course, strictly conform to the Framers' theory of separation of powers.... The anomalous position of administrative agencies in a system of government so deeply committed to the theory of separation of powers has naturally been the subject of intense consideration.[25]

In addition to the perception that broad delegations undermine basic constitutional goals, our attitudes about bureaucracy itself contribute to the illegitimacy of administrative discretion. Students of comparative administration have noted that civil servants do not enjoy the same prestige in America as in other Western nations. Some have hypothesized that this is because highly developed and powerful bureaucracies preceded democratic institutions in Europe, whereas the opposite obtained in the United States. Thus, in Europe, but not America, civil servants enjoyed a traditional legitimacy and prestige in society at a time when people were attempting to reconcile their existence with the concept of representative democracy.[26]

Our lack of faith in bureaucratic expertise also undermines the legitimacy of administrative policy making. This is perhaps especially significant, since the alleged expertise of administrators has served as a primary justification for delegated authority. James Freedman feels that our skepticism about the existence of bureaucratic expertise, or at any rate, about its virtues is due to several factors. It may derive partly from a long-standing distrust of all experts which is inherent in the American character—a trait which may be tied to anti-intellectualism, or to traditional beliefs in pragmatism, common sense, or the equality of man. It may also stem from our strong faith in capitalism and from the perception that public service is a refuge for incompetents unable to compete successfully in the private sector.[27] Finally, doubts about the value of bureaucratic expertise may be due to the growing realization that many of the issues agencies deal with involve broad considerations (including value judgments) which transcend any particular body of specialized knowledge. Many feel that expert judgment can be counterproductive in such instances, leading to policies which emphasize parochial concerns at the expense of broader, more important interests. In this regard, Freedman notes that Americans are sympathetic with Harold Laski's view that "*expertise* consists in such an analytic comprehension of a special realm of facts that the power to see that realm in the perspective of totality is lost."[28]

Our misgivings about delegated authority have been reinforced by a good deal of social science and legal literature which identifies discretion as a source of malaise in the policy-making process. The obvious difficulty of ascertaining legislative intent in the absence of precise statutes notwithstanding, a consistent theme throughout the growing body of implementation studies has been that vague mandates are a key reason for slippage between policy goals and policy outcomes. In reviewing this literature, Frank Thompson observes that

precise policy mandates have had particular appeal. One analysis suggests that given a sound underlying theory a program's prospects improve when "policy objectives are precise and clearly ranked, both internally (within the specific statute) and in the overall program of the implementing agencies." Another study argues "that the surest way to avoid interorganizational implementation problems is to establish a specific mandate and provide sufficient resources...." Yet another hypothesis suggests that policy clarity "is a necessary first step toward effective implementation."[29]

Vague mandates are felt to detract from goal attainment for a number of reasons. Paul Sabatier and Daniel Mazmanian argue that in addition to the fact that they give inadequate substantive guidance to administrators, indefinite legislative directives fail to provide a basis for program evaluation. Institutions with oversight responsibility thus find it difficult to monitor and control the administration of statutes. Similarly, the authors feel that vague mandates are much less useful than clear ones as a strategic resource which those groups who favor program objectives can use to influence the administrative process, either directly or through Congress or the courts.[30] This may be especially significant given that typically there are other groups (and perhaps legislators and bureaucrats as well) with an interest in blocking or changing the thrust of statutory programs as they are being implemented.

Administrative discretion also plays a key role in synoptic accounts of policy failure, especially in the area of regulation. For example, Marver Bernstein states that "in the absence of legislative declaration of goals which regulatory policy should follow, a regulatory agency will function without benefit of political compass and without adequate intelligence or supply lines."[31] In his life-cycle thesis, Bernstein argues that public sentiment in response to a problem caused by unrestrained economic activity eventually builds to the point where Congress is forced to create a new regulatory agency. The accompanying mandate is vague, however, since the legislature finds it impossible to build consensus on specific policies within an inherently conflictual regulatory environment. Because the statute fails to resolve controverted issues, the agency naturally becomes subject to pressures from outside groups. As general public support for its mission declines over time, discretion is used more and more in the service of the regulated groups which the agency was created to control. This is because such interests come to constitute the only viable source of political support for the agency before Congress and elsewhere.[32]

If broad discretion is a natural, if unfortunate, response to political conflict in Bernstein's analysis, others feel that vague mandates are used in a more or less conscious way to pervert the policy process. For example, Murray Edleman argues that the vagueness of most regulatory statutes facilitates their use as symbols. As generally stated intentions to do something, they placate the public, yet at the same time they provide latitude for administrators to do nothing and thus serve dominant economic interests.[33] In perhaps the most popular of all the general indictments of administrative discretion, Theodore

Lowi, Morris Fiorina, Grant McConnell, and others argue that legislators, bureaucrats, and interest group members with intense, complementary interests in particular policy areas secure vague statutes which can be administered in such a way as to serve narrow, "subsystem" goals. According to Lowi, the delegation of authority to "private satrapies" is a central element of "interest group liberalism," a public philosophy which leads to fundamentally incoherent, unjust, and undemocratic governance.[34]

It bears emphasis that misgivings about bureaucratic discretion have not been confined to social scientists and constitutional scholars, but rather have been widespread throughout American society. Furthermore, they have become more salient and intense in recent years as delegated authority has expanded so dramatically. A frequent theme among liberals has been that agencies are overly solicitous of regulated interests. Thus, Richard Stewart states that

the sense of uneasiness aroused by this resurgence of discretion is heightened by perceived biases .... Critics have repeatedly asserted, with a dogmatic tone that reflects settled opinion, that in carrying out broad legislative directives, agencies unduly favor organized interests, especially the interests of the regulated or client business firms and other organized groups at the expense of diffuse, comparatively unorganized interests such as consumers, environmentalists, and the poor.[35]

Such sentiment has been evident in the media, in the halls of Congress, and wherever else public opinion has manifested itself.

Just as regulatory agencies have been attacked for their alleged quiescence by liberals, they have also been criticized intensely for their overzealousness by conservatives. Many have noted that Americans are fundamentally ambivalent on the question of government intervention in the economy.[36] This perhaps explains the fact that, although spawned by popular demands, the health, safety, consumer, and environmental programs created in the 1960s and early 1970s have subsequently precipitated a strong reaction against what have been perceived as excessive and ill-conceived government controls. Administrative agencies have borne most of the criticism, since ultimately they have had to interpret and apply these policies. The reaction against regulation has often led to a questioning of the legitimacy of the administrtive process, as the following excerpts from congressional hearings indicate:

Most of us know that administrative regulations . . . are far reaching and have a tremendous effect on the American people. Oftentimes they go much further than the Congress has ever expected or wanted them to. I know that there is hardly a week that goes by that I don't receive a large number of letters from people in my district complaining about overreaching bureaucracies and about the ways the Federal regulations are affecting their businesses and their lives.[37]

I frankly do not believe that the precepts of a free society are compatible with the situation whereby Congress continues to permit civil servants or appointed officials to conjure up thousands upon thousands of far-reaching laws that can put citizens in jeopardy of liberty or property without anyone elected by the people involved in the process . . . . When an act of Congress contains the pithy section which reads something like this. "The Secretary shall have the power to promulgate regulations to carry out the purposes of this act . . ." —then the citizen is at his peril. . . . the citizen must deal with people unaccountable to him and frequently unresponsive to him.[38]

STRUCTURING ADMINISTRATIVE DISCRETION

The great dilemma posed by administrative discretion, then, is that it is both necessary and problematic. As any viable political system, American government must have the capacity to respond to demands for action. In the interest of effectiveness, the delegation of authority to administrative agencies has thus expanded, and indeed has accelerated, to accommodate modern society's policy needs. If political systems need to be effective, however, they must also exercise authority in a legitimate way. The delegation of discretionary powers to "unaccountable" administrators presents a continual and growing source of tension in this regard, since most Americans feel that policy should be made by officials who are held responsible to the people through the electoral process.

As mentioned in the first chapter, our political system attempts to cope with the tension caused by delegated authority through institutional or constitutional means. We specify the forms and procedures agencies are to use in carrying out statutes in lieu of providing specific substantive policy guidance. As one might expect, the use of structural devices has increased as a function of the magnitude of discretion itself. It was probably not until the 1930s, for example, that delegated authority was sufficiently broad and pervasive as to constitute a source of widespread concern,[39] and not until 1946 that Congress instituted a set of administrative procedures applicable across the federal bureaucracy (after considerable deliberation and a pause of the Second World War). In the area of regulation, the great expansion of delegated authority since the mid–1960s has precipitated a like increase in the use of institutional devices designed to mitigate the problems associated with agency policy making.

Efforts to structure the process of regulatory administration reflect our fundamental political values, as well as our disillusionment with unfettered administrative discretion. To help ensure the accountability of non-elected officials, Congress, the courts, and the executive have each taken significant initiatives to extend their powers to monitor and control agency decisions. Congress, for instance, has often reserved the power to review and disapprove agency actions through the legislative veto in recent years (although the Supreme Court's recent *Chadha* decision [1983] will in all probability preclude the use of most current forms of this device). The courts' oversight of administation has been enlarged along both substantive and procedural dimensions, largely through judical precedent, but also as the result of statutory provisions. Recent presidents have endeavored to extend their control over the administrative process in a variety of ways, including the institution of "analysis review" programs which allow ample opportunities for the executive to examine, influence, and even disapprove proposed regulations.

Aside from (but often in conjunction with) the enhancement of accountability through stronger oversight, administrative institutions have also been intended to promote traditional values in agency decision making, *per se*. The expansion and reinforcement of opportunities for outside parties to participate in the administrative process have been based on the notion that, if broad statutory mandates necessitate policy judgments, then agency decision making should be *responsive*, taking affected interests into account. This development has resulted in part from the perception that agencies have not been sufficiently responsive on their own—that they have become attuned to narrow interests at the expense of broader public concerns. We have also attempted to ensure through devices such as due process requirements and cost-benefit analysis that agency decisions are *rational* or well thought-out—that they are based upon sound interpretations of statutory intent and sound factual premises. In part, these mechanisms reflect our appreciation for the growing technical, social, and economic complexity of the considerations relevant to policy making, together with our doubts about the quality of bureaucratic expertise.

As will become apparent in succeeding chapters, administrative forms and procedures cannot be explained solely as the result of tension between American governmental values and bureaucratic discretion, for they also reflect the efforts of particular interests to gain advantage in the policy-making process. Even in this latter regard, however, arguments are typically couched in terms of traditional normative goals for our political system. In addition, the ostensible rationale behind administrative institutions provides at least one appealing set of criteria for evaluating their effects.

NOTES

1. Kenneth Culp Davis, *Discretionary Justice* (Baton Rouge, Louisiana: Louisiana State University Press, 1969) p. 4.

2. 1 Stat. 28 (1789). Quoted from John P. Comer, *Legislative Functions of National Administrative Authorities* (New York: Columbia University Press, 1927) p. 52.

3. *Ibid.*

4. *Ibid.*, p. 51.

5. James Q. Wilson, "The Rise of the Bureaucratic State," in Frederick S. Lane, ed., *Current Issues in Public Administration* (New York: St. Martin's Press, 1978) p. 30.

6. Murray L. Weidenbaum, *Business, Government, and the Public* (Englewood Cliffs, New Jersey: Prentice-Hall, Inc., 1981) p. 24.

7. *Ibid.*, pp. 8–10.

8. David Mayhew, *Congress: The Electoral Connection* (New Haven: Yale University Press, 1974); Morris Fiorina, *Congress: Keystone of the Washington Establishment* (New Haven: Yale University Press, 1977).

9. The special interests thus favored allegedly reward legislators with monetary and other kinds of political support. The bureaucrats who implement vague mandates under this scenario have an incentive to please committee members by pleasing clientele groups, since the committee members enjoy substantial control over agency budgets and authorizing legislation. For an exposition of this general theme see Theodore J. Lowi, *The End of Liberalism* (New York: W. W. Norton, 1979); Grant McConnell, *Private Power and American Democracy* (New York: Alfred A. Knopf, 1966).

10. Elihu Root in an address to the president of the American Bar Association. 41 *American Bar Association Review* 355, 368–69 (1916). Quoted from Kenneth Culp Davis, *Administrative Law Government* (St. Paul, Minnesota: West Publishing Company, 1975) p. 11.

11. See, for example, David L. Shapiro, "The Choice of Rulemaking or Adjudication in the Development of Administrative Policy," *Harvard Law Review*, 78 (1965) pp. 927–28.

12. Warren E. Baker, "Policy by Rule or Ad Hoc Approach—Which Should It Be?" *Law and Contemporary Problems,* 22 (1957).

13. James M. Landis, *The Administrative Process* (New Haven: Yale University Press, 1938) pp. 23–24. Quoted from James O. Freedman, *Crisis and Legitimacy: The Administrative Process and American Government* (Cambridge: Cambridge University Press, 1978) pp. 44–45.

14. For a good discussion of these and other constitutional issues see Sotrios A. Barber, *The Constitution and the Delegation of Congressional Power* (Chicago: University of Chicago Press, 1975).

15. Robert E. Cushman, "The Constitutional Status of the Independent Regulatory Commissions," *Cornell Law Quarterly,* 24 (1938) pp. 32–33. Quoted from Barber, *supra* note 14, pp. 31–32.

16. Kenneth Culp Davis, *Administrative Law Text* (St. Paul, Minnesota: West Publishing Company, 1973) p. 27.

17. James B. Cheadle, "The Delegation of Legislative Funtions," *Yale Law Journal*, 27 (1918) p. 901.

18. James Hart, *The Ordinace Making Power of the President of the United States* (Baltimore: The Johns Hopkins Press, 1925) p. 41.

19. *Panama Refining Co. v. Ryan*, 293 U.S. 388, 55 S.Ct. 241, 79 L.Ed. 446 (1935); *A.L.A. Schecter Poultry Corp. v. United States*, 295 U.S. 495, 55 S.Ct. 837, 79 L.Ed. 1570 (1935). The more important of these was the famous *Schecter* case, in which the Supreme Court ruled that the National Recovery Act had gone too far in delegating authority to the president "to promulgate codes of fair competition."

20. 143 U.S. 649, 692, 12 S.Ct. 495, 504, 36 L.Ed. (1892).

21. Davis, *supra* note 16, p. 28.

22. Consider the following excerpt from the Marshall Court's *Wayman v. Southard* decision, for example:

It will not be contended that Congress can delegate to the courts or to any other tribunal, powers which are strictly and exclusively legislative. But Congress may certainly delegated to others powers which the legislature may rightfully exercise itself.... The line has not been drawn which separates these important subjects, which must be entirely regulated by the legislature itself, from those of less interest, in which a general provision may be made, and power given to those who are to act under such general provisions to fill up the details.

U.S. (10 Wheat.) 1, 15–16, 6 L.Ed. 263 (1825).

23. Ernst Freund, *Administrative Powers Over Persons and Property* (Chicago: University of Chicago Press, 1928) pp. 14–15.

24. 310 U.S. 381, 389, 60 S.Ct. 907, 914, 84 L.Ed. 1263 (1940).

25. Freedman, *supra* note 13, p. 17.

26. Guy Peters, *The Politics of Bureaucracy: A Comparative Perspective* (New York: Longmans, 1978).

27. Freedman, *supra* note 13, pp. 31–57.

28. Harold Laski, "The Limitations of the Expert," *Harper's Monthly Magazine*, 101 (1930). Quoted from Freedman, *supra* note 13, p. 52.

29. Frank J. Thompson, "Buraucratic Discretion and the National Health Service Corps," *Political Science Quarterly*, 97 (Fall, 1982) p. 428.

30. Paul A. Sabatier and Daniel A. Mazmanian, *The Implementation of Public Policy* (Glenview, Illinois: Scott, Foresman and Company, 1983) pp. 25–30.

31. Marver Bernstein, *Regulating Business by Independent Commission* (Princeton, New Jersey: Princeton University Press, 1955).

32. *Ibid.*

33. Murray Edelman, "Symbols and Political Quiescence," *American Political Science Review*, 54 (September, 1960).

34. Lowi, *supra* note 9.

35. Richard B. Stewart, "The Reformation of American Administrative Law," *Harvard Law Review*, 88 (June, 1975) pp. 684–85.

36. See for example, Freedman, *supra* note 13, pp. 31–35.

37. Walters Flowers (D-Ala.), *Congressional Review of Administrative Rulemaking*. Hearings Before the Subcommittee on Administrative Law and Governmental Relations of the Committee on the Judiciary, U. S. House of Representatives, 94th Cong., 1st Sess., p. 2.

38. Elliot H. Levitas (D-Ga.), Hearings, *supra* note 37, p. 141.

39. Wilson, *supra* note 5.

●3 Rulemaking and Bureaucratic Discretion

The use of rulemaking to guide the subsequent application of policy has been recommended by many students of administration as a way of improving the quality of bureaucratic discretion. Clear rules arguably promote fairness from the perspective of individuals who may be affected by the programs agencies administer. In addition, rulemaking has been advocated as a more forceful, more efficient, and more democratic way for agencies to pursue their mandates. A few have attacked these claims as exaggerations, and even the staunchest advocates of rulemaking have admitted that it is not always an appropriate approach. Nevertheless, there has been a near consensus that rulemaking is desirable in many contexts. Its advantages have been perceived to be especially great in the area of regulation, where it has frequently been compared with case-by-case adjudication as a means of implementation.

Given the advantages claimed for rulemaking, agencies were criticized frequently in the past for their tendency to implement policy in an *ad hoc*, case-by-case fashion. Since the late 1960s, however, the use of rulemaking has been emphasized throughout the federal regulatory bureaucracy. Several factors have contributed to this fundamental change in the administrative process. It is due in part to the fact that some agencies which once relied primarily on adjudication in carrying out their mandates have turned voluntarily to rulemaking. In addition, Congress and the courts have encouraged reliance on rulemaking, and indeed many regulatory statutes enacted in the past fifteen years have required its use.

RULEMAKING IN PERSPECTIVE

Rulemaking and Adjudication

Although forms of administration are probably too numerous and varied to categorize, rules and orders are the two kinds of legally binding directives issued by regulatory agencies. As such, they and the processes through which they are made—rulemaking and adjudication—provide the dominant foci for administrative law. At the same time, however, scholars have been frustrated in their attempts to formulate abstract definitions which neatly separate all formal agency decisions into one or the other of these categories.

As a *substantive* distinction, some authorities define rules as administrative or executive legislation and orders as adjudicatory decisions reached by agencies. Dickinson, for instance, distinguishes a rule (legislation) from an order (adjudication) in the following manner:

What distinguishes legislation from adjudication is that the former affects the rights of individual in the abstract and must be applied in a future proceeding before the legal position of any particular individual will be touched by it; while adjudication operates concretely on individuals in their individual capacity.[1]

The Administrative Procedure Act (APA) contains somewhat similar definitions of the terms "rule" and "order," although it abandons the legislative-judicial analogy.

"Rule" means the whole or part of any agency statement of general or particular applicability and future effect designed to implement, interpret, or prescribe law or policy or describing the organization, procedure, or practice requirements of an agency and includes the approval or prescription for the future of rates, wages, corporate or financial structure or reorganization thereof, process, facilities, applicances, services or allowances therefore or of valuations, costs, or accounting, or practices bearing on any of the foregoing;[2]

"Order" means the whole or a part of a final disposition, whether affirmative, negative, injunctive, or declaratory in form, of an agency in a matter other than rulemaking but including licensing.[3]

The words "or particular" in the APA's rule definition have been a source of confusion. If a statement of particular applicability (that is, one pertaining to a named individual or individuals) which interprets the law is a rule, then what is an order? "Or particular" was not included in early drafts of the act, and it seems apparent from the work of leading scholars of the time that these words violated what was generally understood to be the meaning of the term "rule."[4] Most probably the modification was added to ensure that such marginal activities as ratemaking be defined as rulemaking and thus be subject to the APA's procedural requirements. It is difficult to say precisely what the effect of these words has been, but Kenneth Davis feels that they have not been interpreted in such a way "as to change into rulemaking what before the APA was regarded as adjudication," and that, at any rate, the APA's definition in its entirety has not been taken very seriously.[5] In recent years there has been pressure from the legal profession to amend the APA's definition by deleting "or particular."

Although the notion that rules are abstract statements having future effect and that orders apply to named individuals and have immediate effect seems to be a straightforward distinction, it does not always provide a satisfactory basis for identifying administrative actions. For example, Davis observes that the definition of a rule as an abstract statement means that the legal position of any particular individual cannot be absolutely determined without further adjudicatory action. He then asks the question, "If a rule so clearly applies to X that he obeys it without an enforcement proceeding, and if an injunction is so unclear as applied to Y's activity that Y tests its application in an enforcement proceeding, is the rule or the injunction more abstract or concrete?"[6]

Likewise, Ernst Freund notes that the abstractness of administrative actions can be a matter of degree, and that a gray area exists between what are obviously rules on the one hand and case-by-case actions on the other. As an illustration, he poses a gradation of ratemaking activities which fall on a general-to-particular continuum:

(1) a rate for a particular person for a particular shipment; (2) a rate for a particular person for many shipments; (3) a rate for a particular class of merchandise between two specified places; (4) a mileage rate for a particular class of merchandise; (5) a tariff of charges for a particular road; and (6) a tariff of charges for many roads.[7]

Clearly, (1) represents an instance of case-by-case decision making, while (6) is rulemaking. But at which point does one draw the line between these two extremes?

Perhaps the most severe difficulty posed by a substantive distinction is that, just as the courts, agencies can create policy through adjudicatory precedent. Indeed, orders and the opinions accompanying them have occasionally established very broad standards governing the future application of statutes. For this reason David Shapiro argues that to identify a rule as a statement of general applicability "is to define away the problem, for then all declarations of policy in any form of proceeding become 'rulemaking.'"[8]

Because of the problems which inhere in substantive definitions, many authorities choose to define rules and orders as the results of different administrative processes. For instance, Davis offers the following distinction:

A rule is the product of rulemaking, and rulemaking is the part of the administrative process that resembles the legislature's enactment of a statute. An order is the product of adjudication and adjudication is the part of the administrative process that resembles a court's decision of a case.[9]

Another common distinction, often made implicitly, is that a rule is the product of notice-and-comment proceedings conducted in accordance with the Administrative Procedure Act's rulemaking requirements, whereas an order is a decision reached through the adjudicatory procedures prescribed in the act.

Procedurally based distinctions between rulemaking and adjudication also present problems, however. From a semantic standpoint, it seems illogical to define a rule as the result of rulemaking. More important, procedural definitions are based on the naive assumption that agency decision-making processes can be placed into two reasonably distinct categories. It is difficult to say, for example, just what processes are inherently legislative; certainly the character of congressional decision making varies considerably from case to case. Davis himself observes that most rules are promulgated outside the embrace of the APA and that agency rulemaking procedures are so diverse that they defy categorization. In fact, he seems to contradict his procedural definitions of "rule" and "order" when he argues that the formal due process requirements which sometimes govern rulemaking are inappropriate for what is, in substance, legislative policy making. To the extent that one can define and draw consistent distinctions between the legislative and judicial processes (and this may be difficult), agency decision making may resemble neither or may combine elements of both.

In short, then, one must choose between an imperfect substantive definition of rulemaking and an imperfect procedural one. Although there is substantial precedent for either approach, the former is preferable for the purposes here. Stephen Breyer and Richard Stewart's characterization of rulemaking and adjudication as "useful and familiar paradigms" which admittedly "oversimplify" seems appropriate:

> Rulemaking and adjudication are paradigms of lawmaking whose distinguishing features can be briefly stated. Rulemaking consists in the promulgation of generally applicable requirements or standards governing future conduct. Adjudication consists in determining the legal consequences of past events in a particular controversy between specific parties.[10]

As discussed more fully later in this chapter, these differences between rulemaking and adjudication should be viewed as matters of tendency rather than as absolute distinctions.

Types of Rules

Four general types of rulemaking can be identified for conceptual purposes. The form that shall be of central concern

here can be described as "supplementary" or "legislative." To
borrow from John Comer:

> This class [of rulemaking] involves discretion . . . in framing legis-
> lation for perfecting or elaborating a policy stated in general terms.
> It may be defined as that class of delegated legislation which names,
> or adds to, the administrative law by which the more or less definitely
> stated purpose or policy of Congress is to be carried out.[11]

Supplementary rulemaking thus represents a true delegation
of *legislative authority* from Congress to the president or an
administrative official.

Supplementary rules can be better understood by distinguishing them from what are known as "interpretive" rules.
Interpretive rules are issued to clarify the meaning of statutes,
and as mere translations, they do not create policy in the same
sense that supplementary rules do. Of course, the conceptual
distinction between interpreting and elaborating is as unsa-
tisfying as the notion that judges "discover" the law, and has
given jurists and legal scholars a good deal of trouble. No matter how elusive its theoretical basis, however, the distinction
between supplementary and interpretive rules is of practical
importance for several reasons.

One is that statements designated as interpretive rules do
not have legal force. That is, agencies may not rely on them,
per se, as bases for enforcement proceedings. Rather, interpretive rules serve to advise potentially affected parties of how
agencies will construe statutory language in future situations.
Supplementary rules, on the other hand, do have legal force.
The practical significance of this distinction is that, in regulatory policy at least, supplementary rules save agencies the
trouble of demonstrating the validity of their constructions of
what may be general or vague statutory language in individual
cases, while interpretive rules do not. Also, it is probable that
interpretive rules, because of their advisory nature, do not elicit
the same degree of voluntary compliance as supplementary
rules.

Relatedly, some authorities believe that interpretive rules
are more apt to be overturned by the courts on substantive

grounds, since the judiciary retains the constitutional role as final interpreter of the law. Supplementary rules—which are the law—may not be as vulnerable in this way. Courts may review supplementary rules, but only to determine if they have been made within the scope of statutory delegation, or in some circumstances, to determine if they have been promulgated in accordance with certain legislatively prescribed procedures.[12]

Although there is undoubtedly some truth to this argument, the conceptual distinction between judicial review of an agency's translation of statutory language and judicial review to determine whether or not a rule serves stated legislative goals seems tenuous at best. As a practical matter, moreover, courts have paid a good deal of deference to interpretive rules.[13] Thus, the distinction between supplementary and interpretive rules as to their reviewability may perhaps be viewed most accurately as a matter of degree.[14]

There are two more ways in which the distinction between interpretive and supplementary rules is significant. Agencies need not be authorized by statute to issue interpretive rules (although they often are). Also, the promulgation of interpretive rules is not subject to the procedural requirements established by the Administrative Procedure Act, as discussed in the following chapter.

A third type of rulemaking can be characterized as "contingent." Contingent rulemaking power exists when an agency or the president is authorized to take certain actions pursuant to the occurrence of certain conditions or events. As Comer states, "The contingent class of delegated legislation involves discretion on the part of administrative officials in putting on the active list quiescent or dormant statutes which express congressional policy."[15] James Hart cites the following language from a tariff act passed in 1890 as an example of contingent rulemaking authority:

whenever and so often as the President shall be satisfied that the government of any country producing and exporting ... [designated articles] ... imposes duties or other exactions upon the agricultural or other products of the United States, which in view of the free

introduction of such ... [articles] into the United States he may deem
to be reciprocally unequal and unreasonable, he shall have the power
... to suspend ... the provisions of this act relating to the free introduction of such ... [articles] ... for such time as he shall deem
just....[16]

The element of administrative discretion in the "pure" form
of contingent rulemaking involves only the determination of
whether or not certain conditions exist, and not the creation
or elaboration of law. One should add, however, that the distinction between identifying problems and formulating their
solutions is often an ephemeral one, and at any rate, that contingent rulemaking power can be combined with the discretionary authority to make rules which refine congressional
intent. For instance, the president in the example above was
also given the supplementary authority to specify tariff rates
on formerly duty-free articles.[17]

Finally, it is useful to identify a fourth type of rulemaking.
Contingent, supplementary, and interpretive rules help determine the substance of policy as it is being implemented. One
might say that they put into effect, shape and refine, and trans-
late statutory objectives, respectively. As distinguished from
these, "rules of agency practice and procedure" govern the internal mechanics of the administrative process, and are not
directly concerned with substantive policy output. Of course,
rules of practice and procedure may well affect policy indirectly
by influencing how it is made. For example, the procedures agencies use to promulgate supplementary and interpretive rules,
as well a a variety of other decision-making procedures, are
often the product of this type of rulemaking.

The Legal Basis for Rulemaking

Again, the primary concern here is with supplementary rulemaking—the exercise of legislative authority by administrators. Such rulemaking always takes place pursuant to more
general legislative goals, and is usually expressly authorized
by statutory language which states that the agency shall, at
its discretion, issue rules to achieve certain objectives.

An important qualification, however, is that rulemaking authority need not always be granted explicitly, but is sometimes inferred from a statute. In a number of instances, agencies authorized to issue rules for certain purposes have sought to extend their rulemaking authority to other areas falling within their general jurisdiction, but with respect to which explicit rulemaking authority has not been conferred. Furthermore, the courts have been liberal in upholding these assumptions.[18] In so doing, judges have attempted to justify their decisions in terms of legislative intent. This has been carried off most effectively perhaps in cases where an agency has issued a rule pursuant to some new development which was unforseen at the time its enabling legislation was passed.[19]

At the same time, what the courts have construed as legislative intent in such decisions has supported their notions of good policy. It seems likely, in fact, that policy considerations have often been of foremost importance to the courts in their decisions to uphold assumptions of rulemaking authority, and that justifications in terms of legislative intent have been added *pro forma*. A typical ploy has been to argue that since rulemaking represents a more effective means of achieving a statute's objectives, then Congress must have meant for it to be used in appropriate situations.[20]

The most dramatic affirmation of implicit rulemaking authority was the D.C. Circuit's 1973 decision to uphold Federal Trade Commission rulemaking under Section 5 of the FTC Act. Unlike previous cases, in which agencies had sought to extend rulemaking authority granted for one purpose to other, related areas, the FTC had no express rulemaking authority pursuant to its mission of preventing unfair or deceptive practices. The Court sought to justify its position partly upon the FTC Act's legislative history and partly upon the theory that another section of the statute authorized rulemaking. These rather dubious attempts aside, the Court's remaining rationales were: (1) that rulemaking was a preferable means for implementing policy in some cases, and (2) that the FTC implicitly had rulemaking authority by virtue of the fact that it was expressly granted the power to adjudicate, and that adjudication ultimately produced what were, in effect, rules.[21]

The Choice Between Rulemaking and Adjudication

In many instances regulatory agencies have both rulemaking and adjudicatory powers under their enabling legislation. A widely accepted view is that when such is the case, administrators enjoy the discretion either to promulgate regulations or to pursue their mandates in an *ad hoc* fashion (perhaps developing standards through precedent in the process). The courts have generally upheld agency discretion in the choice between rulemaking and adjudication on the assumption that administrative officials are best acquainted with the problems at hand and are therefore best able to choose the more appropriate tool. The case cited most often in this regard is *SEC* [Securities and Exchange Commission] *v. Chenery*. Although the Supreme Court encouraged the use of rulemaking to develop policy standards in its opinion, it stated that "the choice made between proceeding by general rule or by individual, *ad hoc* litigation is one that lies primarily in the informed discretion of the administrative agency."[22]

Many have criticized regulatory agencies for their tendency to develop broadly applicable standards through adjudication, however, and some have called upon the courts to remedy this problem. At least one scholar feels that there would be strong legal basis for such action. Drawing on the legislative history of the Administrative Procedure Act, William Mayton argues that Congress firmly intended that decisions having general applicability and future effect be promulgated as rules through notice-and-comment rulemaking procedures.[23] The observation that the APA employs a substantive rather than a procedural distinction between rulemaking and adjudication seems to support this view. While the courts have seldom gone this far, several decisions have strongly encouraged the use of rules to state policy. As discussed later, Congress has also prescribed the issuance of rules as a prerequisite for the application of regulatory policy under many new regulatory statutes.

Rulemaking as an Element of Governmental Discretion

Rulemaking can be better appreciated if we consider its role as a means of both exercising and constraining governmental discretion. Hart's distinction between legislative and "individual" discretion is useful in this regard.

Legislation is the discretionary determination of the legal rights and duties of private persons generally, or private persons of a reasonably defined class, and the provision of means of enforcing these rights and duties. By discretion is meant the exercise of choice involving not the scientific application to the facts of objective standards but a subjective evaluation of the advisability of alternatives. The regime of law does not eliminate discretion, but substitutes discretion as to a uniform rule for discretion in individual cases.[24]

Hart's definition of legislation includes both the public laws passed by Congress and administrative rules. Of course, it is simplistic to think that, in most contexts, the exercise of legislative discretion can eliminate discretion in individual cases by reducing administrative decisions to the mere "application to facts of objective standards." But it is accurate to say that the individual decisions made by administrators involve discretion to the extent that they are not guided and delimited by legislation.

In turn, individual discretion is exercised in many ways. Adjudicatory orders and decisions to withhold or bestow government grants, subsidies, services, and the like are obvious examples. Sometimes final determinations pertaining to named individuals are reached through formal proceedings, but much more commonly they are not. This is true even in the area of regulation, where the final disposition of cases is much more frequently accomplished informally rather than through trial-like proceedings. Furthermore, adjudication (either formal or informal) represents only the most visible fraction of all individual discretion exercised by administrators. As Davis states:

Not many questions of discretionary justice ever reach the stage of adjudication, whether formal or informal. Discretionary justice includes initiating, investigating, prosecuting, negotiating, settling, contracting, dealing, advising, threatening, publicizing, concealing, planning, recommending, supervising. Often the most important discretionary decisions are the negative ones, such as not to initiate, not to investigate, not to prosecute, not to deal, and the negative decision usually means a final disposition without ever reaching the stage of either formal or informal adjudication.[25]

Modifying Hart's schema, one can conceptualize a hierarchy of governmental discretion. At the lowest level is discretion exercised in inidividual cases. This sort of discretion is bounded by, takes place pursuant to, and is therefore subordinate to, legislation. Hart's concept of legislation can, in turn, be divided into two hierarchical categories. Congressional legislation (statutory law) authorizes and prescribes the limits for administrative legislation (rulemaking) much as rules constrain individual decisions. (Of course, statutes also control individual administrative decisions in a direct sense in cases where rules have not been issued.)[26]

Rules, then, serve to refine or elaborate the terms of statutes, leaving administrators less leeway in determining to whom statutory provisions apply and do not apply. In areas where agencies administer services, rules define beyond statutory language to whom and for what purposes governmental resources will be allocated. In regulatory areas, supplementary rules go beyond statutory language in proscribing or prescribing individual behavior. As noted, agencies often enjoy the freedom either to issue rules or to apply statutory directives in individual cases, and at any rate they may promulgate rules which are more or less precise. In this sense, the exercise of discretion through rulemaking can be viewed as an alternative to the exercise of discretion on a case-by-case basis.

One should add, however, that a simple dichotomy between rulemaking and case-by-case discretion misses part of reality due to the fact that agencies may establish standards for the future as they interpret legislation in arriving at individual decisions. In this sense, rulemaking can also be viewed as an alternative to adjudication for exercising policy-making discretion. Although there is considerable debate concerning the degree and nature of differences between the two processes, rulemaking tends to be a more comprehensive approach to policy-making, while adjudication tends to establish application criteria in a more incremental fashion. A more detailed discussion of rulemaking and adjudication as policy-making instruments follows shortly.

Finally, it is perhaps appropriate to comment briefly on rulemaking in regards to the policy-making process, since the

view of governmental action as a logical sequence of functions
has become so popular among political scientists as a way of
organizing analysis.[27] According to this perspective, decisions
by legislatures are viewed as policy legitimation—the selection
of a course of action from among alternative approaches to a
problem. In contrast, administrative decisions are typically
lumped together under the rubric of "policy implementation"—
the process of carrying out a course of action that has already
been chosen. Although rulemaking is often referred to here as
a "means of implementation," this is not meant to imply that
it is always or even usually a purely instrumental process. A
general weakness of the process perspective, especially apparent in the case of rulemaking, is that the demarcation between
making and carrying out policy must often be an arbitrary one.
While rulemaking is implementation in the sense that it is
done by agencies, ostensibly in the pursuit of legislative goals,
rules may also reflect broad policy issues which are not addressed
in statutes. Rulemaking often involves the sorts of considerations normally associated with legislation where agency mandates are open-ended.

RULEMAKING AS A MEANS OF
STRUCTURING DISCRETION

Rulemaking has received a good deal of attention as a means
of carrying out statutory mandates. This has especially been
true in the area of regulation, where its use has been viewed
as an alternative to case-by-case adjudication. A frequent theme
has been that a rulemaking approach is salutary in most contexts—that the interests of just and effective government are
served in several respects if agencies exercise discretion through
rulemaking rather than in an *ad hoc* fashion. Important advantages have been claimed for the use of rules, *per se*, in this
regard, as well as for the rulemaking process. At the same
time, arguments for rulemaking have not been accepted without reservation. While many have strongly endorsed its use in
most administrative contexts, some authorities feel that differences between rulemaking and adjudication have been over-

sold or that the latter process is often preferable as a means of carrying out statutory mandates.

Rules and the Rule of Law

Perhaps the most compelling argument for the issuance of rules is simply that it is more just to articulate criteria for administration before statutory programs are brought to bear on individuals. In this sense, rules are said to promote formal justice by precluding or at least mitigating retroactivity, arbitrariness, and capriciousness in the application of policy. As Jeffrey Jowell states:

When argued from the perspective of persons affected by administrative action, the extravagent version of the rule of law maintains that conduct ought to be subject to predetermined rules that will be uniformly applied by officials to all "like" cases. Justice will thus be done in two senses—first as between two or more like-situated parties, who will be treated uniformly, and second, to the extent that persons will not be punished by rules applied *ex post facto*.[28]

Jowell adds that the prospective quality of rulemaking is desirable in a practical as well as an ideal sense—that "a minimum of predetermined knowledge of the legality of our actions is necessary in modern society."[29]

A related virtue claimed for rules is that they promote accountability in administration. This advantage may be singularly important in the United States given the conflict that administrative policy making presents for our political system. To quote Jowell again, the

argument for rules governing administrative discretion reflects a political philosophy that rejects unlimited freedom for the administrative decision maker who is not subject to direct accountability to the electorate. Rules are thus seen as a means of both reducing the free exercise of discretion and providing specific standards against which official decisions may be measured. Where there is no congruence between rule and decision, affected persons could hold officials accountable through challenge by judicial review.[30]

The accountability provided by rules can obviously help ensure against arbitrariness and capriciousness from the individual's perspective. In a broader sense, rules can also facilitate efforts by the public and by other governmental institutions to evaluate administrative policy in terms of legislative objectives or other criteria. This is because the thrust of an agency's policy is apt to be much more visible and straightforward if it is expressed in the form of rules than if it must be distilled from a series of application decisions.

The use of rulemaking in regulatory areas where agencies enforce statutes through adjudication is deemed especially desirable by many writers. The retroactive effects of case-by-case discretion can be severe in regulatory administration, since agency orders bear directly on the rights and duties of individuals and sometimes impose sanctions for actions taken in the past. In this regard, the fact that many regulatory statutes are vague exacerbates the problems presented by an unguided adjudicatory approach. It seems unfair, for instance, to expect those who might be affected by enforcement decisions to divine the practical definitions agencies will give to terms such as "deceptive practice," "unreasonable risk," and the "public interest."[31]

Likewise, the potential for arbitrariness and capriciousness is typically great in the area of regulation. Adjudication often singles out individuals or small groups from large industries, while others engaged in the same or similar practices go unpunished and perhaps continue to reap high profits as a result. The establishment of standards through rulemaking is held up as a hedge against this sort of inequity. As one authority contends, a rule "operates even handedly to bar that practice on the part of all, while an order directed to only one permits his competitors to gain an unfair advantage."[32]

Rulemaking as a More Rational Means of Implementation

In addition to arguments that rules promote formal justice and accountability in administration, rulemaking is widely advocated as a more rational means of implementing policy. Ad-

judication is unique as a form of case-by-case implementation
in that it may create formal criteria for future application decisions through precedent. Thus, it constitutes an alternative
to rulemaking as a tool for developing regulatory policy in
many contexts. In this sense, rulemaking is frequently endorsed as a process which leads to better decisions in several
respects.

A popular argument for using rulemaking to articulate
standards is that it is more effective or forceful than adjudication. One reason for this is that it allows administrators to
formulate and to enforce policy more quickly and with smaller
expenditures of resources. Advocates of rulemaking frequently
contend that standards must be developed incrementally
through a series of proceedings under adjudication, in which
the scope of policy making tends to be limited to the facts
presented by particular cases. Beyond this, they point out that
it may be necessary to bring separate enforcement proceedings
against many individuals for a given precedent to have its
intended effects under adjudication, since orders, like court
decisions, only have direct legal bearing on named parties.
They argue that these same limitations are not present under
rulemaking, which enables agencies to establish broad and
generally applicable standards in a single stroke. Even if those
covered by a rule fail to comply voluntarily with its provisions,
an agency will be faced merely with factual issues in subsequent enforcement proceedings and will not have to defend its
interpretation of statutory law in each new case. The advantages of rulemaking as a more expedient way of achieving
desired policy results are considered to be especially great in
cases where the industry being regulated is large, since the
expense and time required to bring enforcement proceedings
against many firms may prove to be excessive.

Rulemaking is also felt to be more effective than adjudication
because it lends itself more readily to planning and to the
development of coherent, comprehensive standards. For example, James McFarland observes that courts do not select the
issues to be litigated before them, and suggests that "when an
agency acts like a court, it must depend more on the accident
of litigation than on conscious planning."[33] Thus, it may be

difficult under adjudication for an agency to pursue a coherent agenda, even in an incremental fashion. McFarland and others also contend that beyond the fact that adjudication depends on the accident of litigation, it is tied at any rate to the disposition of actual cases. As a result, it does not lend itself to the confrontation of anticipated problems. Rulemaking is advocated as a mechanism which permits a "proactive" approach to policy making in these respects, while adjudication is criticized as essentially a "reactive" tool. The value of rulemaking as a proactive means of regulation is considered to be especially great in areas where there are frequent innovations in technology and industry practices.[34]

Aside from its relative forcefulness, rulemaking is also endorsed as a more sensitive policy-making tool than adjudication. One common argument is that rulemaking allows broader participation and a more comprehensive consideration of decisional criteria. The adjudicatory process, which by its nature centers around named parties, offers respondents extensive opportunities to comment on the legal and factual issues relevant to their guilt or innocence. However, a number of writers maintain that because adjudication focuses with such rigor on the facts relevant to particular cases, it tends to ignore (or at least subordinate to a large degree) comment from other parties who might ultimately be affected by the precedents established through orders. In contrast, rulemaking—as the formulation of administrative legislation—can allow participation by, and can give equal deference to, the entire spectrum of individuals and groups affected by a proposed course of action. In fact, the Administrative Procedure Act's notice-and-comment provisions, which govern most rulemaking in regulatory areas, guarantee that interested parties will have the right to submit written or oral comments on the merits of proposed rules. Rulemaking is thus argued to be a more just approach to policy making which will lead to more enlightened decisions. It is largely because of these perceived virtues that Davis refers to the APA's notice-and-comment procedures as "one of the greatest inventions of modern government."[35]

In what might be viewed as a corollary to these points, Cornelius Peck notes that adjudication may be unfair to named parties in situations where administrators do take into account the broader policy implications of their orders. "If the tribunal in an adjudicative proceeding is too intent on fashioning rules for future guidance, the task of rendering a fair result on the record before it may be slighted.... Consequently, the agency may frequently fail to do complete justice to the parties before it."[36] Accepting the validity of this argument, adjudication must always fall short as a means of making policy. It must either ignore broader interests, or it must do injustice to the litigants in a case. Peck uses several examples of policy making through adjudication by the National Labor Relations Board to illustrate this latter shortcoming.

Rulemaking may also allow for broader decisional input in a qualitative sense. Glen Robinson points out that the informed judgment or expertise of administrators is not as tenable before the courts as a basis for agency actions in adjudication as it is in rulemaking.[37] In addition, Roger Crampton observes that the values and preferences of affected parties, which may be weighed as such in rulemaking, are irrelevant in adjudication. This is esentially because the latter process, with its formal hearings and decision making on the record, tends to limit participation to the presentation of reasoned legal arguments and factual assertions. Crampton feels that the exclusion of such considerations is unfortunate in cases where orders establish broad policies, the premises of which inevitably have normative dimensions.[38]

Moreover, even to the extent that adjudication allows for the consideration of broader policy issues, it may be an inferior means of dealing with them. Davis argues that the adjudicatory process is designed for and suited to the consideration of "adjudicative facts," which "answer the questions of who did what, when, where, how, with what motive or intent." While devices such as discovery, cross-examination, rebuttal, and decision making on the record afford named parties the guarantee of due process on such issues, Davis goes on to argue that these mechanisms are too formal and rigid for the consideration of "legislative facts." Legislative facts "do not usually concern the immediate parties, but are general facts which help to ... decide questions of ... policy and discretion."[39] Speaking from experience as an FTC commissioner, Philip Elman agrees, adding that adjudication often precludes contact between decision makers and agency staff, and that the contentiousness of the process generally stifles the efforts of administrators to "get at the truth."[40]

In sum, then, rulemaking is widely advocated as a more rational means of making policy than adjudication in several respects. It is arguably more comprehensive, since rules have greater breadth and since rulemaking allows for the consideration of a broader range of decisional criteria. Rulemaking is perceived to facilitate planning and coordination in this sense, whereas adjudication is seen as a reactive and potentially disjointed approach to policy making. Rulemaking is also considered to be more rational because it is a more effective (quicker and less costly) means than adjudication for agencies to achieve policy goals, once established.

Qualifying Comparisons between Rulemaking and Adjudication

While arguments in favor of rulemaking enjoy wide currency, they have not been accepted uncritically. Several authorities feel that advocates of rulemaking over adjudication have sometimes confused ideal paradigms of the two approaches with reality. They contend that although the advantages claimed for rulemaking may exist as a matter of tendency, actual differences between it and adjudication have been exaggerated. Another caveat (discussed in the following section) is that important disadvantages can accompany those very features of rulemaking which make it attractive. Case-by-case implementation may have advantages of its own which render it preferable to rulemaking in some contexts.

The most basic counter to arguments for rulemaking is that they confuse form with substance. A point which seems obvious but which is often overlooked by advocates of rulemaking is that rules do not necessarily establish clear standards for the application of policy. Agencies can and sometimes do issue rules which are trivial, which are so vague that they add little to statutory meaning, or which contain a confusing and perhaps inconsistent mass of detail. Of course, bad or ineffectual rules will promote neither justice nor rationality in administration. As an illustration of the latter point, Robinson observes that the Federal Communications Commission has long relied heavily on rulemaking, yet has been criticized often for its failure to plan adequately. He offers the Commission's failure to establish a coherent "deintermixture" policy as a specific example of the fact that rulemaking need not lead to effective policy.[41]

A complementary point is that, just as rules may be trivial, adjudicatory orders may be used to establish important standards. For instance, Shapiro notes that each of the examples of good administration through the articulation of clear standards cited in Judge Friendly's famous lectures occurred through adjudication.[42] Likewise, Shapiro attacks the notion that policy development in adjudication need be an accident of litigation. This may be the case in instances where an agency cannot adjudicate except upon complaint of a private party, or where prosecuting and judging functions are divided between two agencies. The National Labor Relations Board operates under both these constraints, for example. However, many agencies have the power to initiate cases as well as decide them. Shapiro contends that in instances such as these, "agencies can exercise virtually the same degree of planning in the commencement of adjudicatory proceedings as they can in rulemaking."[43]

Of course, the effectiveness of adjudication as a policy-making tool is determined in large part by the degree to which administrators can use orders to articulate standards which go beyond the facts presented by the cases at hand. The more flexibility agency officials have in this regard, the less the potential advantage of rulemaking as an expedient tool for developing policy. Robinson reviews judicial decisions bearing on this issue and concludes that, in Justice Black's words, a standard expressed in an order must be "a legitimate incident to the adjudication of a case before the agency."[44] Robinson feels that agencies have some discretion in formulating general principles which transcend individual cases in the course of adjudication, but he adds that the degree of freedom they enjoy in this regard remains an unsettled question.

As a matter of perspective, it is perhaps best to qualify claims for rulemaking by stating that in practice it tends to offer more potential than adjudication as an effective means of developing policy. Even those who council restraint in comparisons between the two processes generally subscribe to this view. While broad standards can be and sometimes are developed in adjudication, Colin Diver observes that such is typically not the case.

As a way of setting policy, adjudication is customarily, if not instrinsicaly, incremental. The participants' needs circumscribe the decisionmaker's lawmaking role.... In principle, adjudicators can extend policy as much or as little as they wish in a single decision. In practice, however, administrators, like judges, ordinarily attempt to extend policy no further than needed to dispose of the issues at hand.[45]

Arguments that rulemaking elicits broader decisional input than adjudication may also be overdrawn in some respects. As with claims for the relative effectiveness of rulemaking, one should perhaps view its advantages in this regard as a matter of tendency. One relevant point here is that rulemaking proceedings do not always incorporate broad and effective participation. The Administrative Procedure Act's notice-and-comment requirements pertain to regulatory rulemaking and little else. Agencies often fail to solicit input from the public in any systematic way in areas where the act's provisions do not apply and where they are not otherwise constrained by the provisions of individual enabling statutes. Furthermore, even where the APA's procedures do govern rulemaking, they pertain to only a fraction of an agency's total decisional process. Often the most important decisions in the formulation of administrative policy take place well before notice of proposed rulemaking.

In addition, adjudication need not preclude participation by parties who are not involved in the case at hand. Shapiro observes that outside participation in adjudication can occur through a "variety of means ranging from the informal filing of statements or amicus briefs to full intervention by interested parties."[46] Robinson adds that these devices have been augmented by judicial policy liberalizing standing and other rules of intervention in the administrative process. As a result, he feels that "public participation in adjudication has been geatly expanded."[47]

At the same time, however, one should take care not to overstate arguments which depreciate differences in participation under rulemaking as opposed to adjudication. Although broad input from affected interests is not always present in rulemaking, it is at least facilitated by the process. In contrast, even when outside comment is solicited in adjudication, its utility is typically limited by the fact that deciding the case at hand remains the agency's primary responsibility. As Peck observes with regard to the National Labor Relation Board's use of amicus briefs:

It is doubtful that an amicus brief, the arguments of which have been oriented to problems presented in the factual context of a particular case, could approach in value the critical analysis which might have been given to a set of rules covering the multitude of [relevant considerations]. . . .[48]

Moreover, devices such as amicus briefs are optional for agencies and, practically speaking, have been used infrequently.

The Disadvantages of Rulemaking

One general qualification, then, is that the alleged differences between rulemaking and adjudication have been exaggerated to some extent. Another is that it is precisely because of fundamental differences between case-by-case discretion and rulemaking that the former approach is desirable in some contexts. Even the most ardent advocates of rulemaking qualify their enthusiasm in this regard, admitting that detailed standards should not be carried to an extreme. Rules which limit discretion and ensure uniformity in the application of policy may also contribute to administrative inflexibility and may thus impair the pursuit of program objectives in some situations. As Jowell puts it, "Legalism is . . . the prim relative of the unruly arbitrary; they share the quality of a lack of rational relation between the action taken and the ends achieved."[49]

Similarly, "justice may suffer from insufficient individualizing" when discretionary power is too narrow, as no less an advocate of rulemaking than Davis admits.[50]

Based on these realizations, a common theme among students of administration is that reliance on rulemaking should be determined by contextual factors. For example, an agency may not possess the knowledge required to issue rules, due perhaps to its newness or to the newness or complexity of the problems it must confront. A wise approach in such instances may be to proceed cautiously on a case-by-case basis until the experience needed to draft a sound rule has been acquired. As former SEC chairman William Cary notes:

In many situations, an agency's experience with a particular problem is too limited to allow for meaningful rule making. Complex policy decisions, moreover, can sometimes best be formulated by focusing on one aspect of a broad problem at a particular time.[51]

Similarly, Warren Baker observes that the "first impression or reaction to a matter often turns out to be quite erroneous" and that an incremental, adjudicatory approach can allow an agency to "build its commitments gradually, and even to change its mind."[52] In fact, there may be areas in which rulemaking is "never feasible, even after the accumulation of considerable experience." Shapiro cites the NLRB's mandate to ensure that unions bargain in "good faith" to illustrate his point. He feels that little can be added to this statutory command—that the "ultimate question in each case . . . must remain the subjective good faith of the bargaining agent."[53]

Just as detailed rules may sacrifice individual justice and effectiveness in the ill-advised pursuit of evenhandedness, the rulemaking process may in a sense dilute the quality of participation in the interest of broad decisional input. As Robinson states:

To expand participation appreciably beyond those who have a distinctive interest or those who can make a significant contribution may add to the democratic character of the process, but this may not be worth what it costs in efficiency to review the volumes of irrelevant or marginally useful commentary that sometimes descends upon the

agency from such an invitation.... The very facet of rulemaking ...
which is applauded for permitting broad participation may serve as
well to keep the depth of involvement and the treatment of specific,
complex issues shallow.[54]

A virtue claimed for adjudication is, of course, that it affords
extensive opportunities for participation by those who are most
directly and immediately affected by agency decisions. Moreover, the viability of participation in the adjudicatory process
is guaranteed to an extent by various procedural rights and by
the stipulation that agency decisions can be well reasoned and
based on a formal record. Another contextual consideration
relevant to the use of rulemaking may therefore be the number
of persons who stand to be affected intensely by an agency's
policy as compared with the number of persons who stand to
be affected in a more marginal way. Adjudication may be a
preferable course where the former group is small and the latter
large.

THE USE OF RULEMAKING BY
REGULATORY AGENCIES

The Reluctance of Agencies to Issue Rules in
the Past

Notwithstanding the qualifications that may apply to arguments in its favor, there has long been a near consensus
among students of the administrative process that the use of
rulemaking to guide individual decisions is desirable in most
contexts. Indeed, the notion that agencies did not rely on rulemaking heavily enough had reached the status of conventional
wisdom by the late 1960s. Federal regulatory agencies, which
typically enjoyed the discretion to issue rules as they saw fit,
were considered to be especially guilty of proceeding in an
unguided, case-by-case fashion when considerations of good
administration seemed to warrant a rulemaking approach.
Kenneth Davis was the leading (but by no means the only)
academic exponent of this view. As he wrote in 1969:

The typical failure in our system that is correctable is not legislative
delegation of broad discretionary power with vague standards; it is

the procrastination of administrators in resorting to the rulemaking power to replace vagueness with clarity.... American administrators ... have fallen into habits of unnecessarily delaying the use of their rulemaking power. They too often hold back even when their understanding suffices for useful clarification through rulemaking.[55]

The same sentiments were expressed in important government commission studies, in judicial opinions, in congressional hearings and reports, and elsewhere. For example, a 1960 congressional report on the independent regulatory commissions was highly critical of the injustice inherent in their *ad hoc* approach to implementation. It stated that a fundamental problem in regulation was the "discriminatory enforcement of law and regulations," which was due in part to the "failure to formulate or to publicize policy and interpretations so that the regulated industry is kept timely informed of the rules of decision."[56] Another report issued in the following year lamented the inefficiency of the adjudicatory approach to regulation often used by agencies. It cited delay as "the most critical problem in the field of government by commission" and listed the "lack of clearly defined and publishable standards and policies" and the "lack of planning for future ... developments in the industries being regulated" as foremost among the factors contributing to "mounting backlogs."[57]

Though the subject received surprisingly little attention given its perceived importance, several explanations were offered for the reluctance of agencies to issue rules in "instances in which the principles of sound administration would suggest, if not dictate, resort to rulemaking proceedings."[58] The most popular was that agencies were simply unwilling to make the hard choices among competing interests which were necessary in order to establish clear and binding policy standards. For example, Pendleton Herring argued in 1936 that if considerations of sound administration dictated rulemaking, political expediency often dictated otherwise.

The task of interpretation is a continuation of the legislative process. The full implications of this should be faced. Independent commissions are called upon to give substance to a vague congressional mandate by establishing rules and regulations. They are subject to the same pressures that assailed the legislators.[59]

J. Skelly Wright echoed this thesis as a practical critique of Davis' prescription for more rulemaking. To support his argument, Wright cited a number of instances in which agencies had been attacked by aggrieved interests as the result of their attempts at broad rulemaking and ultimately had suffered rebuke at the hands of Congress or the courts.[60] Similarly, William Cary noted in *Politics and the Regulatory Agencies* that

in the field of rulemaking by commissions pursuant to statutory authority, Congress is often likely to interfere.... The result is that much of the effort ... resembles the launching of trial balloons, only to find them punctured by a congressional committee. The common technique of a committee or its chairman who opposes a proposed rule is to say that the Commission has exceeded its authority.[61]

Cary substantiated this observation with anecdotes from the FCC and other agencies.

The thesis that rulemaking was avoided as too bold a commitment jibed well with pluralist political theory which viewed policy making as a response to the pressures exerted by conflicting and often shifting coalitions of interests. It was more prudent in this regard for agencies to retain discretion, fashioning compromises on a case-by-case basis as the political exigencies of the moment demanded. The commitment-avoidance explanation also agreed with the complementary notion that government decision making could not be comprehensive and rational in most contexts and was of necessity, therefore, an incremental process.

A second explanation offered for the avoidance of rulemaking was that it constituted a more forceful means of implementing statutes. According to some authorities, agencies were not constrained so much by the need to maintain flexibility in coping with political conflict as they were by the need to please the regulated interests who dominated their policy-making environments. Industry was basically opposed to government control under this scenario, and agencies therefore adopted case-by-case adjudication because it provided extensive due process rights for affected parties and, relatedly, because it was a slow and ineffective means of regulation. Adjudication enabled administrators to appear busy while having minimal effect on industry practices. Thus, Marver Bernstein devoted a chapter to administrative adjudication in developing his "capture" thesis.

The growth of passivity in the process of regulation by commission tends to dilute and eventually destroy the assertion of regulatory initiative by the commissions. The comforts afforded by judicialized procedure and the role of administrative tribunal are more highly regarded by commissions than searching for the public interest in regulatory policies, winning the consent of the regulated to a vigorous program of regulation, and enforcing regulations in a manner which deters violations and maintains the integrity of the program.[62]

A complementary explanation for the tendency of agencies to avoid rulemaking was that the resulting lack of codification made the thrust of policy (or non-policy) less visible. The passiveness of administrators was therefore less likely to arouse concern among the general public (which was ostensibly being served) and its representatives.

A third, very different explanation for the reluctance of agencies to issue rules was offered by James Wilson. Rather than viewing this phenomenon as the result of constraints placed on agencies by their environments, he argued that administrators were primarily motivated to exert control over those they regulated, and that bureaucratic power was, in turn, a function of the ability to behave arbitrarily in making individual decisions. Therefore rulemaking, which limited case-by-case discretion, was avoided as a vitiation of agency power. Illustrating this with an analogy, he stated:

the greater the codification of substantive policy, the less power the agency can wield over any client in the particular case.... In a baseball game the umpire has power because he can call me out after three strikes; but his power over me would be much greater if every time I came to the plate he told me how many strikes I would be allowed depended on how well I swung the bat, or maybe on how clean my uniform was.[63]

   In addition to these explanations, which equated the failure to issue rules with an unwillingness to articulate standards, Shapiro speculated that agencies might prefer adjudicatory precedents over rules as a form of policy—that "considerations, perhaps felt but not fully perceived,... may lead an agency to conclude that it is safer to rely on other means for the announcement of important policies."[64] One explanation offered by Shapiro was that adjudication permitted agencies greater opportunity to apply new policy to prior conduct. Another was that a standard developed through an adjudicatory proceeding might be better able to withstand judicial review than the same standard issued as a rule. This was because a reviewing court might disagree with the reasoning behind an order (which would establish policy for future decisions), but might also agree with the agency's finding and thus sustain its decision. The same policy articulated as a rule would be overturned on its merits.

   A final explanation offered by Shapiro was that agencies enjoyed greater freedom to depart from adjudicatory precendents in future decisions than from rules. "By eschewing [rules] in favor of the declaration of [standards] by adjudication, an agency is likely to regard itself as freer, and will in fact be given greater freedom by the courts, to ignore or depart from those [standards] in specific instances without giving sufficient reasons."[65] Shapiro argued that the desirability of ajudication as a means of establishing less-binding policy was especially great where agencies were faced with uncertainty, due perhaps to a lack of technical knowledge or to an unstable political environment. Obviously, this explanation complemented the notion that rulemaking (*qua* standard setting) was avoided as an impolitic commitment.

The Rulemaking Revolution

   If agencies were inclined to proceed on an *ad hoc* basis in the past, however, they have dramatically changed their approach to implementation in recent years. Rulemaking has been emphasized throughout the federal regulatory bureaucracy, as Antonin Scalia notes:

The 1970s have been aptly described by expert observers of the federal administrative process as the "era of rulemaking." To an astounding degree, a system which previously had established law and policy through case-by-case adjudication involving parties—whether in licensing, ratemaking, or enforcement proceedings—began setting forth its general prescriptions in rules, leaving little to be decided in subsequent adjudications beyond the factual issues of compliance or noncompliance with the rules....[66]

The "rulemaking revolution" has had several immediate sources. Established agencies, which at their discretion formerly emphasized adjudication, have turned voluntarily to rulemaking as a means of developing new policy and codifying precedent from past cases. Relatedly, increased emphasis on rulemaking in areas where its use has traditionally been optional has been encouraged from without. Colin Diver notes that the judiciary's role in this regard has been significant.

The courts ... threw their weight behind the greater use of rulemaking. Instances of judicial insistence on rulemaking, though rare, accumulated rapidly enough to provide rulemaking enthusiasts like Kenneth Culp Davis the basis for discerning a general tendency. Courts invoked a variety of legal grounds—due process, organic statutes and internal agency procedures, or abuse of discretion—for divining an obligation to proceed by rulemaking. Some cases merely vacated specific agency orders as inadequately justified, while others directly commanded the agency to initiate rulemaking proceedings.[67]

Likewise, rulemaking has sometimes come at the behest of Congress. As discussed in Chapter 5, for instance, much of the FTC's heightened rulemaking activity in the late 1960s and 1970s was the result of legislative prodding.[68]

Beyond the encouragement of rulemaking, its use has been mandated by most of the important new regulatory legislation in the areas of health, safety, and the environment. Thus, in carrying out most of their responsibilities, the Occupational Safety and Health Administration, the Consumer Products

Safety Commission, the Environmental Protection Agency, and the National Traffic Highway Safety Administration are required by their enabling statutes to issue rules before actions can be brought against individuals. In addition, recent statutes have often included "action forcing" provisions which have required agencies to issue rules to achieve certain regulatory goals within a specified period of time. By requiring rulemaking, mandates in the area of "social" regulation have imposed a markedly different approach to administration than the "economic" regulatory legislation of the past.

Students of administration have suggested several underlying explanations for the rulemaking revolution. Certainly, the widespread advocacy of rulemaking as a just and effective means of implementation may have had some effect. In a related sense, Colin Diver feels that the recent emphasis on rulemaking is one practical manifestation of a fundamental change in orientation within the American political system. He argues that the dominant conceptual model of policy making generally and of the administrative process particularly used to be one of "incrementalism." This view held that the most prudent way to develop policy was through marginal additions or adjustments. Faced with limited knowledge and political conflict, decision makers should proceed slowly, dealing successively with small parts of larger policy problems. If adjudication fit well with the incrementalist model, however, it was antithetical to the "new consensus about policy making" which according to Diver began to emerge in the mid–1960s and attained dominance in the early 1970s. As "comprehensive rationality" came to replace incrementalism as a guiding paradigm, the advantages of rulemaking as a means of soliciting broad decisional input and of dealing with whole problems at once became more appealing.[69]

Beyond abstract considerations of good administration, some suggest that the rulemaking revolution reflects the interests of various actors in the political system. Stephen Breyer and Richard Stewart feel that the expendiency and effectiveness of rulemaking as a means of achieving regulatory goals have made it increasingly attractive to agencies as their workloads have increased.

Recently there has been a dramatic shift toward greater use of rulemaking by many agencies.... this shift is less attributable to the persuasiveness of the commentators who have championed rulemaking than to resource constraints and other factors that have made rulemaking comparatively more attractive from the viewpoint of bureaucratic self-interest.[70]

Also, it may be that the encouragement and requirement of rulemaking by Congress and the courts has come largely as the result of disillusionment with agency performance in the past, and as an effort to ensure the attainment of statutory goals in the future. As mentioned, the traditional adjudicatory approach to implementation came to be viewed by some as a convenient means by which agencies had avoided their regulatory responsibilities. As a relatively ineffective means of regulation, adjudication was seen to facilitate passiveness by agencies which were perhaps reluctant to displease regulated interests. As a relatively less visible means of implementation, adjudication may have even been viewed as something which facilitated actions favoring regulatees at the expense of the public interest. Thus, in explaining the rise in popularity of action forcing requirements under which agencies must issue rules, Bruce Ackerman and William Hassler state that

it is asserted that the agencies had somehow failed to make use of their broad rulemaking powers to engage in creative policy making in the public interest. They had relapsed instead into the old lawyer-ridden ways of case-by-case adjudication, laboring mightily through procedural labyrinths without successfully defining basic directions for future regulation.[71]

CONCLUSION

Rulemaking has been widely advocated as a means of implementing policy. Although arguments for rulemaking have not gone unqualified or unchallenged, it has generally been endorsed by students of administration as a means of constraining discretion in individual cases and as a means of formulating more rational, more democratic, and more forceful policy. Despite the advantages claimed for rulemaking, agencies were often disinclined to use it in the past. Since the late 1960s, however, there has been a growing emphasis on rulemaking throughout the federal regulatory bureaucracy. While there is a large literature dealing with rulemaking from an administrative perspective, much less has been written about its political significance. How is an agency's use (or nonuse) of rulemaking influenced by, and how does it subsequently affect, an agency's relationship with its political environment? Several authors have addressed these questions, as mentioned, but they have typically done so in passing and have offered relatively little empirical support for their speculations. This book is intended in part to help fill this void. Chapters 5 and 6 examine FTC rulemaking in the context of that agency's relationship with "those external actors who are interested in its operations and able to render support or bring about sanctions."[72] As discussed in the concluding chapter, the FTC's experience is likely instructive in regards to the political causes and effects of the rulemaking revolution.

NOTES

1. Quoted from Kenneth Culp Davis, *Administrative Law Text* (St. Paul, Minnesota: West Publishing Company, 1973) p. 3.
2. 5 U.S.C.A. sec. 551 (4)
3. 5 U.S.C.A. sec. 551 (6)
4. See, for example, James Hart, "The Exercise of Rulemaking Power," *Report of the President's Committee on Administrative Management* (Washington, D.C.: U.S. Government Printing Office, 1937) pp. 313–22.
5. Davis, *supra* note 1, pp. 229–30.
6. Davis, *supra* note 1, p. 228.
7. Ernst Freund, *Administrative Powers Over Persons and Property* (Chicago: University of Chicago Press, 1928) p. 64.
8. David L. Shapiro, "The Choice of Rulemaking or Adjudication in the Development of Administrative Policy," *Harvard Law Review*, 77 (March, 1965) p. 924.
9. Davis, *supra* note 1, p. 228.
10. Stephen G. Breyer and Richard B. Steward, *Administrative Law and Regulatory Policy* (Boston: Little, Brown and Company, 1979) p. 398.

11. John P. Comer, *Legislative Functions of the National Administrative Authorities* (New York: Columbia University Press, 1927) p. 27.

12. As Justice Connor stated in one Supreme Court decision:

When administrative rule-making is based on clear authority from the legislature to formulate policy in the adoption of regulations, the rulemaking activity takes on a quasi-legislative aspect.... In the federal system, when an administrative agency is clearly acting in its quasi-legislative rule-making capacity, the United States Supreme Court has not substituted its judgment as to the content of the rule or regulation. On the other hand, when it appears that the adoption of a regulation concerns merely the interpretation of a statute, the United States Supreme Court may give the agency's interpretation weight, but such interpretation is not controlling.

Skidmore v. Swift & Co., 323 U.S. 134, 65 S.Ct. 161, 89 L.Ed. 124 (1944). Quoted from Davis, *supra* note 1, p. 320.

13. Davis, *supra* note 1, pp. 230–31.

14. *Ibid.*

15. Comer, *supra* note 11, p. 30.

16. 26 Stat. L., 567, ch. 1244. Quoted from James Hart, *The Ordinance Making Power of the President of the United States* (Baltimore: The Johns Hopkins Press, 1925) pp. 48–49.

17. *Ibid.*

18. For a good discussion see the opinion of J. Skelly Wright, *National Petroleum Refiners Association v. FTC* 482 F.2d 672 (1973).

19. For example, in upholding an extension of its rulemaking authority by the Federal Power Commission, one judge stated:

All authority for the Commission need not be found in explicit language. Section 16 [the FPC's general statutory rulemaking provision] demonstrates a realization by Congress that the Commission would be confronted with unforseen problems of administration in regulating this huge industry and should have a basis for coping with such confrontation. While the action of the Commission must conform to the terms, policies, and purposes of the Act, it may use means which are not in all respects spelled out in detail.

Pub. Services Comm'n. of State of New York v. FPC, 117 U.S. App. D.C. 195, 199, 327 F.2d 893, 897 (1964).

20. The quotation in note 19 illustrates this, as does the following excerpt from another important decision:

Since the Commission, unlike a court, does have the ability to make new law prospectively through the exercise of its rulemaking powers, it has less reason to rely on *ad hoc* adjudication to formulate new standards of conduct within the framework of the Holding Company Act. The function of filling in the interstices of the Act should be performed, as much as possible, through the quasi-legislative promulgation of rules to be applied in the future.

SEC v. Chenery Corp., 332 U.S. 194 (1947).

21. Wright, *supra* note 18. Several writers have attacked these arguments. See, for example, Robert Weston, "Deceptive Advertising and the FTC," *The Federal Bar Journal*, 24 (June, 1964).

22. *SEC v. Chenery, supra* note 20.

23. William Mayton, "The Legislative Resolution of the Rulemaking Versus Adjudication Problem in Agency Lawmaking," *Duke Law Journal* (1980).

24. Hart, *supra* note 16, pp. 48–49.

25. Kenneth Culp Davis, *Discretionary Justice: A Preliminary Inquiry* (Baton Rouge, Louisiana: Louisiana State University Press, 1969) p. 22.

26. Comer extends this hierarchy even further, arguing that rulemaking is subordinate to statutory law in much the same way that the latter is subordinate to the Constitution. As he states, "Just as a large part of congressional legislation results directly from the "necessary and proper" clause of the Constitution, so ... [rulemaking] is a direct result of the secondary "necessary and proper" clauses of the statutes under which it issues." *Supra* note 11, p. 26.

27. See, for example, Charles O. Jones, *An Introduction to the Study of Public Policy* (North Scituate, Massachusetts: Duxbury Press, 1977). Jones divides the policy-making process into five stages: problem identification (demand for government action to resolve a problem), formulation (proposal to resolve a problem), legitimation (the adoption of a proposal as a program), implementation (applying the program), and evaluation.

28. Jeffrey L. Jowell, *Law and Bureaucracy: Administrative Discretion and the Limits of Legal-Action* (Port Washington, New York: Dunellen Publishing Company, 1975) p. 12.

29. *Ibid.*, p. 13.

30. *Ibid.*, p. 12.

31. Warren Baker cites the FCC's issuance of rules governing reserved broadcast time contracts to illustrate the value of rulemaking as a means of avoiding retroactivity. The Commission's reliance on adjudication in this policy area aroused criticism for its "destruction of private interest," which was effectively quelled when the agency promulgated rules establishing clear contract standards. Warren E. Baker, "Policy by Rule or Ad Hoc Approach-Which Should It Be?" *Law and Contemporary Problems*, 22 (1957) p. 662.

32. The FTC's statement of basis and purpose of Trade Regulation

Rule regulating cigarette advertising, *Federal Register*, 29 pp. 8325, 8367.

33. James McFarland, "Landis' Report: The Voice of One Crying Out in the Wilderness," *Virginia Law Review*, 47 (1961) p. 433.

34. Lee Fritschler's study of the FTC's attempts to regulate ever-changing advertising claims by cigarette manufacturers through adjudication and the agency's subsequent adoption of rulemaking illustrates the futility of the former approach and at least the perceived effectiveness of the latter. A. Lee Fritschler, *Smoking and Politics* (Englewood Cliffs, New Jersey: Prentice-Hall, 1969).

35. Davis, *supra* note 25, p. 65.

36. Cornelius Peck, "The Atrophied Rulemaking Powers of the National Labor Relations Board," *Yale Law Journal*, 70 (1961) p. 756.

37. Glen O. Robinson, "The Making of Administrative Policy: Another Look at Rulemaking and Adjudication and Administrative Procedure Reform," *Pennsylvania Law Review*, 118 (1970) pp. 519–20.

38. Roger C. Crampton, "The Why, Where, and How of Broadened, Public Participation in the Administrative Process," *Georgetown Law Review*, 60 (1972) pp. 527–32.

39. Kenneth Culp Davis, *Administrative Law Treatise* (St. Paul, Minnesota: West Publishing Company, 1958) sec. 7.02.

40. Philip Elman, "Rulemaking Procedure in the FTC's Enforcement of the Merger Law," *Harvard Law Review*, 78 (1964) p. 390.

41. Robinson, *supra* note 37, pp. 535–39.

42. Shapiro, *supra* note 8, p. 920.

43. *Ibid.*, p. 932.

44. Robinson, *supra* note 37, p. 509.

45. Colin S. Diver, "Policymaking Paradigms in Administrative Law," *Harvard Law Review*, 95 (1981) p. 403.

46. Shapiro, *supra* note 8, pp. 930–33.

47. Robinson, *supra* note 37, p. 515.

48. Peck, *supra* note 36, p. 756.

49. Jowell, *supra* note 28, p. 15.

50. Davis, *supra* note 25, p. 52.

51. William L. Cary, *Politics and the Regulatory Agencies* (New York: McGraw-Hill Book Company, 1967) p. 131.

52. Baker, *supra* note 31, p. 662.

53. Shapiro, *supra* note 8, pp. 927–28.

54. Robinson, *supra* note 37, pp. 515–16.

55. Davis, *Discretionary Justice, supra* note 25, pp. 56–57.

56. *Investigation of Regulatory Commissions and Agencies*, House Report No. 1258, 9 February 1960, p. 5.

57. *Independent Regulatory Commissions: Report of the Special Committee on Legislative Oversight of the House Interstate and Foreign Commerce Commission*, House Report No. 2238, 3 January 1961, p. 42.

58. Shapiro, *supra* note 8, p. 942.

59. Pendleton Herring, *Public Administration and the Public Interest* (New York: McGraw-Hill Book Company, 1936) p. 218.

60. J. Skelly Wright, "Beyond Discretionary Justice," *Yale Law Journal*, 81 (January, 1972).

61. Cary, *supra* note 51, p. 45.

62. Marver H. Bernstein, *Regulating Business by Independent Commission* (Princeton, New Jersey: Princeton University Press, 1955) pp. 293–94.

63. James Q. Wilson, "The Dead Hand of Regulation," *The Public Interest*, 25 (1971) p. 51.

64. Shapiro, *supra* note 8, p. 942.

65. *Ibid.*, p. 951.

66. Antonin Scalia, "Back to Basics: Making Law Without Rules," *Regulation Magazine* (July/August, 1981) p. 25.

67. Diver, *supra* note 45, pp. 409–10.

68. Also see William F. West, "The Politics of Administrative Rulemaking," *Public Administration Review*, 42 (1982).

69. Diver, *supra* note 45.

70. Breyer and Stewart, *supra* note 10, pp. 403–4.

71. Bruce Ackerman and William Hassler, "Beyond the New Deal: Coal and the Clean Air Act," *Yale Law Journal*, 89 (1980) p. 1474.

72. Harold Stein defines an agency's political environment in this way in "Public Agencies as Political Actors," in Frederick S. Lane, ed., *Current Issues in Public Administration* (New York: St. Martin's Press, 1978).

•4 Structuring Rulemaking Discretion

As agencies' reliance on rules has expanded, both in an absolute sense and in relation to other means of implementation, the rulemaking process has also become more highly structured. Administrators were usually left to their own devices in formulating rules until 1946, when the Administrative Procedure Act imposed notice-and-comment requirements on most regulatory rulemaking. Further, even the APA's procedures were intended merely to provide useful information for agencies rather than to guide or delimit their decisions. It is in marked contrast to earlier policy, therefore, that Congress, the courts, and the executive have instituted a variety of procedural requirements for rulemaking which place significant constraints on administrative discretion.

THE ADMINISTRATIVE PROCEDURE ACT

Pressures to Reform the Administrative Process

The amount and scope of discretionary authority delegated to administrators began to take off dramatically in the late 1800s and early 1900s. Perhaps most significant in this regard were the broad legislative and adjudicatory mandates given to agencies for essentially the novel purpose of economic regulation. Between 1887 and 1935 agencies were empowered to regulate railroads, trusts, foods and drugs, standards of fairness in commerce, broadcasting, securities, and a variety of other things.[1]

The growing importance of administrative policy making had become a widespread source of concern by the late 1920s. Many, of course, objected to delegated authority, *per se*, as a violation of constitutional principles and as an otherwise unsound practice. Beyond this, there was a growing sense of discontentment with the administrative process. Given the reality of delegated authority, there were often no procedural standards which prescribed how the quasi-legislative and quasi-judicial responsibilities of agencies were to be carried out. A few enabling statutes did specify administrative procedures: for example, some agencies were required to meet with designated group representatives or to hold public hearings before issuing rules, and some were required to use trial-like procedures in arriving at decisions involving individuals. By and large, however, safeguards such as these were missing. Procedures were typically left to the discretion of administrative officials and varied greatly among agencies as a result. They also varied in an *ad hoc* fashion within individual agencies, which often failed to formulate and publicize guidelines standardizing their own decision-making processes. The frustration one scholar expressed in 1927 attests to the chaotic state of the administrative process at the time.

> Just what the procedure is in any particular department or special agency at one time is difficult to get at; departmental practices are not for the outsider. A governmental employee ... sometimes gives a glimpse of what actually happens. Usually such glimpses, since they are given with an initial cautiousness and a finger-on-the-lip sign, are of little documentary value. Few departments give freely.[2]

Dissatisfaction with the administrative process mounted during the 1930s and early 1940s and eventually culminated with the passage of the Administrative Procedure Act in 1946. Proponents of reform during this period were not of a common mind, however. One camp, the most important members of which were the legal profession and the business community, chafed at the delegation of legislative and judicial authority to bureaucrats—at least beyond that which was absolutely necessary. This sentiment was due in part to the belief that such grants violated the separation of powers principle. Perhaps more importantly, conservatives correctly perceived that delegated authority was an essential element of regulation and of "big government" in general. They realized that it was ultimately bureaucracy which infringed upon individual freedoms and interfered with the sound operation of the free enterprise system.[3] The following passage from a popular book published in 1932 summarizes the feelings of many of those who had become dismayed by the growth of administrative power:

Uncle Sam has not yet awakened from his dream of government by bureaucracy, but ever wanders further afield in crazy experiments in state socialism. Possibly some day he may awaken from his irrational dreams, and return again to the old conceptions of government as wisely defined in the Constitution of the United States.[4]

Others, however, took a much more sanguine view of the exercise of legislative and judicial power by bureaucrats. The most articulate sopkesmen for this latter group might be loosely described as New Deal intellectuals. To them, broad delegations of authority were necessary if government was to cope with society's needs. In addition, they felt that delegation was often salutary because it enabled administrators to bring their expertise to bear on public problems. Congress and the courts typically lacked the time or the training to deal with the complex issues generated by modern society. The report of the Brownlow Committee, for example, reflects these views.

The tradition in favor of statutes is a perversion of a principle that is fundamental to the system of government in the United States. Nobody questions the principle that the basic policies of government must be embodied in the statutes of Congress. But it does not follow from this—indeed it is both unhistorical and unsound to hold—that Congress must state in minute detail either its basic policies or the administrative methods by which they are to be carried out.... The

practice of delegating rulemaking authority to administrative agencies represents the adaption of eighteenth century governmental machinery to twentieth century governmental problems.[5]
  . . . by constantly rubbing elbows with their particular problems,
administrators are in a peculiarly advantageous position to attain an
intimate and specialized knowledge, born of experience which gives
them a "sense of what is practically enforceable" and enables them
to "plan a program of development."[6]

Not surprisingly, the proposals offered by those who feared
and those who welcomed bureaucratic discretion differed considerably, and there ensued a long period of conflict over how
the administrative process should be reformed. As has usually
been true in the choice of administrative institutions, the debate which preceded the Administrative Procedure Act was
expressed in terms of differing normative and empirical prop-
ositions concerning bureaucracy, its capabilities, and its proper
role in government. As is also typically the case, however,
conflict stemmed in part from competing interests who perceived
that the choice of procedure would ultimately have important
substantive policy implications.

The American Bar Association (ABA) appointed a special
committee on administrative law which in 1934 began issuing
annual reports and proposals for reform. The thrust of these
recommendations was to limit administrative discretion as much
as possible. In 1939 the ABA sponsored the Walter-Logan Bill,
which would have placed severe constraints on administrative
action. The following excerpt from supporting testimony before
the House Judiciary Committee by the president of the ABA
captures the tenor of the bill's provisions:

Congress is the legislative branch of government . . . and we do not
any longer want Congress to set up bureaus and commissions and say
to them: "We recognize there is a great problem in this particular
field. We have not the time to solve this problem as we did in the
early days of this Republic; we are merely going to set up a commission
of some kind and give you full powers and you endeavor to solve that
problem."[7]

Essentially, Walter-Logan would have limited agency discretion by imposing judicialized procedures on practically all agency

actions and, relatedly, by strengthening the courts' oversight of those actions. Under threat of review, agencies would have been required to hold hearings and to justify decisions—whether licensing, final orders, intermediate orders, rules, etc.—on the basis of "substantial evidence" or the "facts contained in the record."[8] The Walter-Logan Bill passed both houses, but was vetoed by President Roosevelt. In 1938 FDR had requested the attorney general to appoint a committee to investigate the need for reform in administrative law. As his justification for vetoing the Walter-Logan Bill, Roosevelt stated, "I should desire to await their [the attorney general's committee] report and recommendations before approving any measure in this complicated field."[9] It is safe to assume, of course, that Roosevelt was never in doubt concerning the desirability of the Walter-Logan Bill. In large part this legislation was an attempt by conservatives indirectly to emasculate his New Deal programs by limiting the ability of administrators to act.

In his message accompanying the Walter-Logan veto, Roosevelt also stated that the purpose of the attorney general's committee was not to hamper administration, but to "suggest improvements to make the process more workable and more just."[10] The *Final Report* issued by the committee in 1941 generally reflected this goal. The committee's majority felt that sweeping standardization of procedures was unwise, since agency actions were diverse and took place within a wide variety of contexts. Instead, they "emphasized the need for continuing study and piecemeal reform" of the administrative process.[11] The legislative proposal which accompanied the report was concerned almost exclusively with the standardization of procedures for adjudicatory actions which were required by existing statutes to be made after a hearing and based upon a record. With respect to rulemaking, the bill merely sought to impose uniform requirements for the publication of final regulations. (A minority on the attorney general's committee did favor more-stringent and far-reaching procedures, however, and proposed separate legislation which bore many similarities to the Walter-Logan Bill.)[12]

World War II delayed the legislature's further consideration of proposals for administrative reform, but in 1946 a compromise was finally struck which resulted in the Administrative Procedure Act. Which side came out better in the bargain is a matter of controversy. Several accounts of the act argue that lawyers and their industry clients clearly won the day.[13] For instance, Foster Sherwood states that "the statute as finally written bears close resemblance to earlier plans formulated by [the American Bar Association and the minority of the attorney general's committee]."[14] Similarly Frederick Blachly and Miriam Oatman conclude their article entitled "Sabotage of the Administrative Process" by noting that the APA is "based . . . upon the desire of lawyers to have maximum opportunity to participate in the process of administration, to block administrative action, and to subject the administrative process to judicial methods and judicial controls at every point."[15]

Others, however, feel that the APA was, on the whole, a victory for those who accepted bureaucracy's prominent role in modern government and who were thus reluctant to impede administrative performance with unduly burdensome procedural requirements. In the views of Davis, Freedman, and others, the act reflected a relatively sanguine attitude about bureaucratic discretion and was based in large part upon the majority recommendations of the attorney general's committee.[16] Congress' designation of the committee's *Final Report* as the APA's official legislative history is used to substantiate this latter point.

Differing assessments of the APA may be attributable in part to differences in the backgrounds and perspectives of those who wrote them. For example, students of government or public administration are more likely to view due process requirements as burdensome than are legal commentators, who are apt to consider such procedures indispensable in many contexts as a prerequisite for just and responsible action. In a related sense, disparity among accounts of the act may be due in part to differing focal points. The APA does impose rigorous, trial-like procedures in instances where enabling legislation requires adjudicatory decisions to be "determined on the record after an opportunity for an agency hearing." Marver Bernstein is referring to this when he states that the act "symbolizes the hostility of the legal profession" toward administrative regulation.[17] As discussed below, however, the act's rulemaking procedures are much less constraining. It is largely in this sense that the APA stands in marked contrast to the Walter-Logan Bill and other proposals which would have imposed judicialized procedures and strict standards of review upon agencies' quasi-legislative activities as well.

Rulemaking Requirements of the Administrative Procedure Act

The APA regulates the administrative process in a number of ways. It specifies when and how certain types of agency output and internal operating procedures must be publicized. It also establishes criteria for assigning all formal administrative actions to either of two categories—rulemaking or adjudication—and sets forth agency procedures and terms of judicial review to be used in each case. The concern here, however, is with the act's rulemaking requirements.

The APA stipulates that agencies publish in the *Federal Register* all "substantive rules of general applicability." The only rules exempted from this requirement are (1) those "authorized ... by an Executive order to be kept secret in the interest of national defense or foreign policy," (2) those "related solely to the internal personnel and practices of an agency," (3) those "specifically exempted from disclosure by a statute," and (4) those "involving privileged or confidential trade secrets and commercial or financial information." Aside from these exceptions, rules not so published are not legally binding, except in certain circumstances where individuals are notified in some other manner.[18]

Rules which must be published in the *Register* do not become effective until thirty days after they appear there. The only exceptions to this requirement are rules which grant or recognize exemptions from other federal regulations, interpretive rules, and rules that, for good cause, an agency feels should go into effect before thirty days have elapsed. In this last instance, a statement of the agency's rationale for waiving the thirty-day requirement must accompany its published rule.

Most importantly, the APA also establishes two sets of procedures for developing rules. The two formats are widely referred to as "informal" and "formal" rulemaking, although the act itself does not employ these or any other descriptive terms. Informal requirements, which can be viewed as the APA's standard format, apply to the general exercise of rulemaking power. They are superseded by formal procedures only when "rules are required by statute to be made on a record after opportunity for an agency hearing." Although there has been a good deal of controversy as to just what statutory phrases trigger formal requirements, as a practical matter they have been used infrequently.[19]

Under informal requirements (set forth in Section 553 of the APA), agencies must give public notice that a rule is being contemplated and must provide some means by which interested parties may express their views concerning the proposed action. (For obvious reasons, then, informal procedures are also commonly referred to as "notice-and-comment rulemaking.") Section 553 stipulates that, with certain broad exceptions, notice be published in the *Federal Register*, and that it include "(1) a statement of the time, place, and nature of the public rulemaking proceedings; (2) reference to the legal [statutory] authority under which the rule is proposed; and (3) either the terms or substance of the proposed rule or a description of the subjects and issues involved." This last requirement means that, at the very least, notice must indicate that an agency is contemplating making policy in a particular area to confront certain alleged problems or needs. The legislative history of the APA encourages agencies to be as specific as possible at this stage as a way of focusing subsequent comment, and in practice, notices often contain definite proposals.[20]

Agencies must solicit written comment under informal rulemaking and may also hold public hearings if they wish. The framers of the APA clearly perceived that while input from interested parties could have salutary effects, efforts to obtain such information could also be costly in terms of time and agency resources. Past the minimum requirement of written comment, the appropriate balance between expediency and public participation was considered to be a contextually bound determination best left to agency discretion.²¹ The APA further instructs agencies to consider relevant comments in formulating their final decisions. No mechanisms are provided to ensure that administrators consider comments, however, aside from the vague provision that courts may overturn rules determined to be "arbitrary or capricious." Final rules must be accompanied only by a "concise general statement of their basis and purpose."

In sum, the APA's informal procedures reflect the notion that rulemaking is legislative in character. For the process to be democratic and well informed, therefore, administrators should be exposed to the views of the affected public. In its report on the APA, the Senate Judiciary Committee quoted the report of the attorney general's committee approvingly in this regard.

An administrative agency . . . is not ordinarily a representative body. . . . Its deliberations are not carried on in public and its members are not subject to direct political controls as are legislators. . . . Its knowledge is rarely complete, and it must always learn the . . . viewpoints of those whom its regulations will affect. . . . [Public] participation . . . in the rulemaking process is essential in order to permit administrative agencies to inform themselves and to afford safeguards to affected interests.²²

At the same time, however, informal rulemaking reflects a basically positive attitude about bureaucratic discretion and an unwillingness to constrain agency officials with excessively rigorous and inflexible procedural requirements.

Whereas informal rulemaking is said to bear many similarities to the legislative process, formal rulemaking is often described as quasi-judicial. Indeed, the latter format, defined in Sections 556 and 557 of the APA, is much the same as that prescribed for adjudication. Hearings are mandatory under formal rulemaking, and must be conducted like courtroom proceedings, with the swearing of witnesses, the taking of depositions, and rulings on offers of proof and the relevancy of evidence. The burden of proof is on the proponent of the rule (usually the agency), and parties are entitled to present their cases through oral or documentary evidence, to submit rebuttals, and to conduct cross-examination. Perhaps the most salient feature of formal rulemaking is that decisions must be based explicitly and exclusively on the record, which consists of the hearing transcript and any written comment and/or evidence submitted before, during, or after the hearing.

There may be several reasons for the existence of both formal and informal rulemaking procedures in the APA. It has been suggested that informal rulemaking, like the legislative process, is flexible and well suited for making decisions which involve value considerations and other broad policy judgments. In contrast, formal rulemaking, like the judicial process, may have certain advantages in dealing with narrower questions of fact. For example, an agency charged with regulating the prices of certain commodities in accordance with specified parameters of supply and demand might use formal procedures in evaluating the testimony of economists, bureaucrats, industry officials, consumers, and other witnesses. Relatedly, the *Final Report* of the attorney general's committee suggests that formal rulemaking may also be appropriate when it is clear in advance that certain narrow interests will benefit or suffer if a proposed regulation is issued. In such cases, the due process provided by formal procedures may be desirable as a protection of individual rights.[23]

Whatever the merits of these ostensible rationales, Robert Hamilton notes that formal procedures have been prescribed by Congress for rulemaking ranging from that based on narrow factual issues to that involving broad, value-laden considerations. As an example of the former, the Agricultural Marketing Service uses formal procedures to make rules establishing prices for various commodities. Its decisions turn on essentially narrow questions such as, What is the likely yield of a certain crop from a certain area during a particular period of the year? As an illustration of the latter, the Food and Drug Administration uses formal procedures to regulate the advertising and labeling of various types of products. Often, its decisions involve considerations such as, What *should be* the standards required for a product to be legally advertisable under a given generic name?[24]

The APA's prescription of two rulemaking formats may be

better explained as the product of conflict over the desirability of administrative policy making. Informal rulemaking reflects the view of liberals of the era that the exercise of legislative authority by administrators is necessary and desirable. The information-gathering processes prescribed in Section 553 are similar in some ways to those used by congressional committees. Hearings—if they are held—are conducted in an inquisitorial rather than an adversary manner. Likewise, comments received in informal rulemaking are intended as an aid which the agency can use or ignore at its discretion.

Formal procedures reflect a much more skeptical view of administrative policy making. The premises for formally made rules are treated as assertions of fact, logic, and law which may be challenged in an adversary setting and which the agency must substantiate in the record. Courts may overturn rules not so justified, as well as rules felt to have been promulgated without scrupulous regard for the procedural rights of affected parties. Formal procedures may well have been included in the Administrative Procedure Act as a concession to conservative, anti-delegation interests—as a readily available constraint that could be imposed upon agencies in those policy areas where opponents of regulation could mount sufficient pressure.

Clearly, the attorney general's committee envisioned informal procedures as the standard format for rulemaking in regulatory areas and formal procedures as an infrequent constraint. In practice this has been the case. Davis observes that formal rulemaking procedures are only prescribed in about sixteen statutes, the most important of which is the Federal Food, Drug, and Cosmetic Act of 1938.[25]

Exemptions from the APA

Although the APA applies to all agencies in the abstract, its procedures actually govern only a small percentage of all federal rulemaking. This is primarily because broad substantive classes of rules are exempted by the act from its notice-and-comment requirements. The following types of rules need not entail notice and comment:

- rules relating to the military or foreign affairs functions of the United States
- rules relating to agency management or personnel
- rules relating to public property, loans, grants, benefits, subsidies, or contracts
- interpretive rules
- general statements of policy
- rules of agency organization, procedure, or practice

For good measure, APA procedures are not required "when the agency for good cause finds . . . that notice and public procedure thereon are impracticable, unnecessary, or contrary to the public interest."

Some reasons for these exemptions are explicit in the legislative history of the APA, and others seem obvious. Interpretive rules were excluded because they are not legally binding. Congress also felt that, as the interpretation rather than the elaboration of statutory policy, such rulemaking would be subject to a higher degree of judicial control than substantive rulemaking. Thus, it did not warrant the same procedural safeguards.[26] Rules concerning personnel and management and rules of organization, procedure, and practice were exempted because they deal solely with internal agency matters and, as such, do not directly affect the public. Congress expressed the desire to encourage the issuance of such rules, and reasoned that notice-and-comment requirements would cause undue delay in many cases.[27]

Rules relating to foreign and military affairs were exempted because in some cases notice and comment would violate national security or render timely decision making impossible. Also, many such rules, while perhaps having substantive policy effects, do not directly affect U.S. citizens. Finally, rules relating to public property, loans, grants, benefits, and contracts were most probably exempted because the framers of the APA felt these classes of decisions affected the distribution of government largess and therefore involved privileges rather than rights and duties. Thus, citizens were not entitled to the same participatory guarantees as in regulatory rulemaking.

Most of the exemptions from notice-and-comment requirements have been accepted as legitimate on the whole. In each case, however, there has been some concern that a blanket exception is too broad—that public participation is desirable for certain definable types of rulemaking in the area. The exemptions which have received the most criticism are those for public property, loans, grants, benefits, and contracts. A number of respected authorities, as well as the Administrative Conference of the United States, have recommended that these exceptions be deleted from the APA. Critics have attacked the artificiality of the rights-versus-privileges argument, marshalling recent court decisions to support their position. They have also noted that loans, grants, benefits, and contracts represent a very sizeable portion of the federal budget, and that the public has a tremendous material interest in the rules which establish criteria for the allocation of such goods.[28]

The Voluntary Adoption of Notice and Comment

The legislative history of the APA indicates that exemptions were conceived as classes of rulemaking in which it *might* not be appropriate to use notice and comment. Congress felt that it was necessary to ensure that agencies were not indiscriminately bound by procedural requirements in these areas. Nevertheless, the framers of the act believed that much rulemaking within the excepted categories could be improved by notice and comment, and encouraged agencies to use informal rulemaking whenever practical. As the House Judiciary Committee's report on the APA states, none of the act's blanket exemptions "is to be taken as encouraging agencies not to adopt voluntary public rulemaking procedures where useful to the agency or beneficial to the public. The exceptions merely confer a complete discretion upon agencies to decide what, if any, public rulemaking procedures they will adopt in a given situation within their terms."[29]

Despite this encouragement, agencies were very reluctant to adopt APA procedures voluntarily in the first twenty-five years following the act's passage. A questionnaire distributed by the

House of Representatives in 1957 indicates that, at the time, agencies seldom used informal procedures in situations where they were not required to do so.[30] Another, less widely distributed survey sent out by the Senate in 1968 reveals approximately the same thing.[31] These studies show that rules were often promulgated without any attempt to solicit the views of interested parties, and that where such attempts were made, they often fell short of the APA's informal requirements in terms of comprehensiveness. For example, some agencies reported that they occasionally notified and engaged in informal consultation with whomever they happened to think appropriate under the circumstances.[32]

The questionnaires reveal several typical agency explanations for their reluctance to employ notice and comment. Perhaps the most common was that APA procedures imposed an undue administrative burden. Another was that the agency was doing quite well in representing the public interest without using notice and comment. In this regard, some agencies indicated that their policies affected only a few groups and individuals with whom they consulted regularly on an informal basis.

If agencies not constrained by the APA tended to avoid notice and comment before 1970, however, there appears to have been a significant increase in the voluntary use of informal procedures in the past decade or so. Table 4.1, which presents a sampling of the *Federal Register* at three points in time, shows a dramatic rise in the ratio of proposed rules to all rules. Writing in the late 1950s and again in the late 1960s, Davis estimated that perhaps no more than 20 percent of all federal rulemaking was subject to APA constraints.[33] Accepting this, the data in the table support the impression rendered by the 1957 House survey that notice and comment was seldom used voluntarily. By 1968 the relative incidence of informal procedures had risen some, but the great increase appears to have occurred since then. While some of this increase undoubtedly resulted from requirements imposed by individual enabling statutes, most of it is likely attributable to agency initiative.

The apparent increase in the use of notice-and-comment procedures by federal agencies is part of a larger trend that has

Table 4.1
Rules and Proposed Rules

	Decem- ber 1958	Decem- ber 1968	Decem- ber 1978	Decem- ber 1982
Rules	286	433	504	480
Proposed Rules	58	123	247	296
Ratio: Proposed Rules/ All Rules	20.3	28.4	49.0	61.6

Note: Agency business which appears in the *Register* is published under the headings "Notices," "Rules and Regulations," and "Proposed Rules." Notices alert the public to agency actions other than rulemaking. Rules and regulations consist of the final rules promulgated by agencies. Most rules are required to be published in the *Register*, regardless of the procedure used in their promulgation. On the other hand, almost every entry under "Proposed Rules" represents a notice of proposed rulemaking and an invitation for public comment. Therefore, one can obtain a fairly accurate idea of the extent to which notice-and-comment procedures are used by comparing the number of proposed rules over a given period with the number of rules and regulations.

This design is open to the criticism that proposed rules represent policy that will be finalized several months (or perhaps years) hence. Therefore, the numbers in the "Proposed Rules" column are not components of the respective figures in the "Rules" column. The approach used here is probably fairly accurate, however. Using pages in the *Federal Register* as a rough index, it does not appear that rulemaking activity is consistently higher at some times of the year than at others. At any rate, the ratios, all taken for months of December, are useful for examining relative differences in the use of notice and comment over time.

Of course, one must also assume that the ratio of *regulatory* rulemaking to all rulemaking has remained stable (or at least has not grown dramatically) if these figures are to be used to support the contention that the voluntary use of notice and comment has increased. This is probably an accurate assumption. Although many new regulatory statutes were enacted during the 1970s, and although rulemaking became more popular as a regulatory device, there was a tremendous expansion of government activity in other areas as well.

occurred at all levels of government. As one authority noted in 1978:

Recent years have witnessed an increase in the number of official participation programs employed by administrative agencies. In the last eight years alone, there have been more than 25 hearings in Congress focusing on the need for greater public participation in federal agency proceedings, and participation has become part of every major federal domestic program. City governments have put into practice a wide range of participation structures, and the outpouring of citizen-complaint bureaus, little city halls, and citizen advisory committees, to cite only a few examples, has been impressive indeed.[34]

The growth in popularity of mechanisms designed to increase citizen input in the administrative process is generally attributable to heightened enthusiasm for participatory democracy in the 1960s and 1970s. As mentioned, this enthusiasm led to a good deal of criticism of some of the APA's exemptions and to an Administrative Conference recommendation that Congress extend the act's informal requirements to rules concerning public property, loans, grants, benefits, subsidies, and contracts. The Department of Health, Education, and Welfare alluded to this recommendation and its underlying rationale when, in 1971, it required all of its constituent agencies to use notice-and-comment procedures in formulating such rules.

Our implementation of the Conference's recommendation should result in greater participation by the public in the formulation of this Department's rules and regulations. The public benefit from such participation should outweigh the administrative inconvenience or delay which may result from the use of the APA procedures in the five exempt categories.[35]

The Effects of Notice-and-Comment Procedures

The purpose of informal procedures is to ensure that administrative decisions are informed by the views of affected members of society. Comment can provide agency officials with valuable factual input, as well as information concerning the preferences of relevant individuals and groups. Beyond this, the provision of meaningful opportunities to participate in the administrative process can help legitimate agency decisions. Although some have assumed that notice-and-comment procedures have these salutary effects (Davis' oft-cited claim that informal rulemaking is "one of the greatest inventions of modern government" again comes to mind),[36] relatively little evidence has been collected which bears on the effectiveness of APA procedures in achieving their intended results. Several writers have taken a critical look at notice-and-comment rulemaking, however, and have suggested that its virtues have been oversold.

Three conditions must be fulfilled in order for notice and comment to work as designed. Obviously, potentially affected individuals and groups must be aware that an agency intends to promulgate a rule as a precondition for effective participation in administrative policy making. A limitation of APA procedures is that the *Federal Register*—the standard means of providing notice—is a voluminous, cumbersome document which few Americans know about, much less read. Furthermore, monitoring the *Register* involves costs which not all elements of society can bear with equal ease. Arthur Bonfield observes that the poor and/or disorganized are especially prone to be disadvantaged in these regards, and argues that the APA's rulemaking procedures are generally biased in favor of middle-class and business interests.[37]

To an even greater degree than the cost of staying informed, the cost of effective participation can also limit public input and thus contribute to decisional bias. At the very least, effective participation demands the expenditure of time and effort in preparation. Such investments can be considerable in complex or technical proceedings. In addition, substantial monetary costs are typically involved in rulemaking. In 1972, for instance, an Administrative Conference study found that attorneys' fees in Food and Drug Administration rulemaking often exceeded $100,000, and that expert witness fees for Interstate Commerce Commission (ICC) ratemaking sometimes totaled $40,000 or $50,000.[38] After observing that privately owned electric and gas utilities spent more than $38 million in administrative proceedings in 1974, Bruce Frederickson and his colleagues asked rhetorically if consumer groups could conceivably have afforded similar efforts.[39]

Finally and perhaps most importantly, an agency's receipt of comment is no guarantee that its ultimate decision will reflect the views expressed by affected interests. As mentioned, the intent behind informal rulemaking was merely to ensure that agencies be *exposed* to relevant views. Thus, the APA itself is lax in its provisions concerning agency response to public comment (although judicial interpretations of the act have changed this considerably in recent years, as will be discussed in the next section). Surprisingly, there has been little if any systematic effort to examine the effects of public comment on agency decision making.

An observation which has led several writers to express pessimism concerning the significance of participation in rulemaking proceedings is that APA procedures typically constrain only a fraction of an agency's decisional process. As William Pederson writes: "The Administrative Procedure Act is only a statute; it is not the source of all agency procedures. Commentators who focus too narrowly on the APA may forget what lies behind it, and the long paths an agency rule may have to trace before even being proposed for comment."[40] Pederson's study of the Environmental Protection Agency indicates that the brunt of evidence collection, consultation with affected groups and other agencies, and policy formulation takes place *before* notice of proposed rulemaking, and that the agency is generally satisfied that it has heard all of the relevant comments it is going to hear and that it has made all of the modifications in its rule that it should make at the time informal proceedings begin. Similarly, Lee Fritschler observes in his case study of the Federal Trade Commission's cigarette rule that

hearings themselves serve some useful and important purposes. However, one of these purposes does not seem to be changing the viewpoints of any of the participants.... With the considerable amount of time that went into the preparation of the cigarette labeling case ... there was little factual information that the commissioners did not have at their disposal. Backed by the scientific evidence of the Surgeon General's report and the detailed work of their own counsel's office, the commissioners seemed fairly certain as to what the outcome of the hearings would be.[41]

Formal Procedures as an Alternative

Some have viewed the APA's formal rulemaking as a means of guaranteeing the effectiveness of participation through trial-like hearings. If simple notice-and-comment procedures have been criticized as ineffectual, however, formal rulemaking has been attacked by a number of administrative law scholars as a process which imposes costs far more onerous than are warranted by any benefits they might confer. Robert Hamilton has done the best empirical work on this subject. In his case studies on the Food and Drug Administration and other agencies, he finds that formal procedures have stalled the promulgation of rules for years in many cases. Hamilton attributes delay to protracted trial-like hearings and, relatedly, to the records upon which decisions must be based. He notes, for example, that one hearing concerning the labeling of diet foods involved over two hundred days of testimony and produced a transcript of 32,000 pages. The author adds that such administrative burdens also impose a tremendous drain on agency resources, and that their ultimate effect may be to discourage agencies from issuing rules.[42]

In addition, Hamilton, Davis, and others contend that for all of the effort expended in formal proceedings, there are few if any accompanying benefits in most contexts. Indeed, it is claimed that due to their rigidity, formal procedures actually inhibit effective treatment of the sorts of issues which typically arise in rulemaking. Davis, for instance, argues that while trial-like procedures are appropriate for dealing with questions of adjudicative fact (who did what, when, where, how, and with what motive or intent), they are ill-suited for the consideration of legislative facts. Rather, he feels that informal, give-and-take discussions lend themselves much better to the consideration of the sorts of future possibilities upon which policy decisions are usually based.[43]

In view of the burdens they impose, Davis expresses relief that formal procedures are used infrequently in rulemaking. "Even though trials on questions of policy and on questions of broad or general fact are procedural monstrosities and are far too numerous in an absolute sense, they affect less than one percent of all rulemaking."[44] As discussed below, however, it has become inaccurate to view informal procedures as the dominant paradigm for rulemaking among federal regulatory agencies. To an increasing extent in recent years, Congress and the courts have seen fit to impose rulemaking procedures which fall somewhere in between the formal and informal poles defined in the APA.

PROCEDURAL REQUIREMENTS BEYOND THE APA

Although the APA provides the foundation for the administrative process, it is far from the only source of rulemaking procedure in the federal bureaucracy. Enabling statutes, judicial opinions, and executive orders have imposed a variety of requirements which supplement or supersede those of the APA. Efforts to structure the exercise of quasi-legislative discretion have become especially popular over the past twenty years in the area of regulation, where delegated authority has expanded dramatically, and where rulemaking has become increasingly popular as a means of exercising such discretion. If rulemaking is perceived to be fairer and more effective than adjudication, it is also a more precipitous and forceful means of regulation. Given this, Congress, the courts, and the executive have become dissatisfied with simple notice-and-comment requirements as the sole constraint on agency discretion.

Efforts to structure rulemaking have been informed by either or both of two general objectives. One has been to improve the exercise of bureaucratic discretion in an intrinsic sense through procedural constraints more rigorous than simple notice-and-comment rulemaking. The other has been to increase the accountability of the rulemaking process by enhancing the abilities of Congress, the courts, and the president to monitor and control agency decisions.

Hybrid Rulemaking Procedures

Perhaps the most important development in administrative rulemaking in recent years has been the imposition of judicialized procedures by Congress and the courts. Since the mid-1960s, Congress has frequently shown its reservations concerning administrative policy making by attaching "hybrid" procedures to new delegations of authority. These requirements derive their name from the fact that they represent a compromise between the APA's formal and informal rulemaking. Although they vary considerably in their details from agency to agency, hybrid procedures typically require administrators to hold hearings and to base final rules on the evidence contained in a record. In many cases, they also confer opportunities for cross-examination and rebuttal, sometimes under the proviso that hearing officers may restrict the exercise of these rights to single parties representing groups with substantially the same interests. Hybrid procedures reflect the realization that informal rulemaking provides few assurances that agencies will consider relevant comments and arrive at reasoned decisions, as well as a lack of faith, perhaps, that administrators will do these things if left to their own devices. Yet hybrid procedures also reflect the fear that full, trial-like hearings will stifle the administrative process.[45]

Hybrid requirements have been included with most new delegations of authority to regulate consumer products, advertising and labeling, safety, and the environment. The following is a partial list of statutes enacted since 1965 which require rulemaking on the record (and in most instances cross-examination and rebuttal):

Section 201(u) of the Federal Food, Drug, and Cosmetic Act

Federal Metal and Nonmetallic Safety Act

National Traffic and Motor Vehicle Safety Act

Fair Packaging and Labeling Act

Flammable Fabrics Act

Federal Coal Mine Health and Safety Act

Comprehensive Drug Abuse Prevention Control Act

Occupational Safety and Health Act

Magnuson-Moss Warranty-Federal Trade Commission
     Improvement Act

Toxic Substances Control Act

Consumer Products Safety Act

As an extension of this trend, recent legislative proposals would amend the APA to require cross-examination and decision making on the record for all regulatory rulemaking. A broad administrative reform bill containing such a provision was passed unanimously by the Senate in the Ninety-seventh Congress.[46]

Judicial policy has paralleled that of Congress in the area of rulemaking procedure. Spurred by the Supreme Court's 1971 *Overton Park* decision,[47] a series of circuit court precedents in the 1970s contemplated that administrators operating under the APA's informal requirements base rules on well-defined records as a prerequisite for meaningful judicial review, and later that agencies also incorporate adversarial elements of due process in their proceedings. Many commentators feel that the effect of these decisions has been to transform the "arbitrary and capricious" standard of review found in Section 553 of the APA into something which closely approximates the more stringent "substantial evidence" criterion used in formal rulemaking.

Although the Supreme Court's 1978 *Vermont Yankee* decision ostensibly repudiated attempts by lower courts to impose procedures which went beyond the language of the APA, there is a near consensus that it did not erase these earlier developments.[48] The decision itself was contradictory, since it also stated that the courts should review rulemaking on the basis of an evidentiary record and that simple notice-and-comment procedures would sometimes be inadequate for creating such a record. (The APA's Section 553 does not mention rulemaking records, and agencies typically did not create them—at least formal ones—during notice-and-comment proceedings.) In the most comprehensive treatment of *Vermont Yankee* and its effect on earlier policy, Stephen DeLong states: "The Court did not intend to go so far as to return to pre-*Overton Park* rulemaking. Justice Renquist's opinion reaffirmed the importance of a record supporting a decision and the reviewing court's authority to require additional justification for the agency decision, two doctrines at the core of hybrid rulemaking cases."[49]

A natural accompaniment to *Overton Park* and its progeny has been the restriction of *ex parte* communications in order to ensure a better record for the purpose of substantive review.

The precise nature of this new stricture remains unclear: one important D.C. Circuit case seems to envision an absolute proscription, while subsequent decisions by the same court have allowed off-the-record contacts between agency officials and outside parties in some contexts. Whatever its extent, however, the new limitation on *ex parte* communications represents a important break with past practice. Traditionally, off-the-record contacts were prohibited in formal adjudication, but were unrestricted in notice-and-comment rulemaking and other types of informal proceedings.[50]

Hybrid rulemaking procedures have been designed to serve several objectives. One, evinced in both judicial opinions and congressional documents, has been to increase the accountability of agencies to the courts. Unlike the APA's notice-and-comment procedures, the requirement that decisions be based on a well-defined record which has been tested through the adversary process provides a basis upon which judges can evaluate the rationale behind agency actions. As Paul Verkuil states:

> The Supreme Court's opinion in *Overton Park* signaled a new era in judicial review. At issue was a definition of the scope of review contemplated by the "arbitrary or capricious" standard of the APA.... The Court held that the administrative record that was before the Secretary must be presented to the reviewing court to enable it to undertake its independent evaluation.[51]

Hybrid procedures have also been intended to improve the quality of agency rulemaking in important respects. One purpose behind such requirements has been to ensure that agency decisions are rational, or well thought-out. Cross-examination, rebuttal, and decision making on the record have been designed to force agencies to develop sound factual, logical, and legal linkages between their proposed actions and legislative intent. Decisions not so justified may be overturned by the courts. As the House report on the Consumer Products Safety Act states, for example: "Commission rules are to be overturned unless each of the findings which the Commission is required to make ... is shown to be supported by "substantial evidence" on the record taken as a whole. Thus, ... determinations are subjected to [a] stricter standard of review [than under the APA's informal procedures]."[52]

Another common justification for hybrid procedures has been that the APA's notice-and-comment requirements provide no assurance that the views and arguments of affected interests will be registered. Hearings are optional under this format, and when used, are conducted in an informal, legislative manner. Opportunities for affected parties to challenge regulations are also limited, since courts have little basis for review in the absence of a record. In contrast, hybrid procedures often afford interested parties opportunities to challenge agency premises through cross-examination and the submission of competing studies and testimony. Furthermore, agencies are compelled to respond adequately to such challenges under threat of a much stricter standard of judicial review. Thus, the House report cited above also states that

the [APA's] informal procedures were not thought to provide the desired opportunity for interested parties to participate in the Commission's rulemaking proceeding.... The committee has accordingly crafted an administrative procedure to be employed in this bill which it believes will maximize opportunities to participate in the rulemaking proceedings....[53]

Expanding Influence over Agency Rulemaking

Aside from the imposition of hybrid procedures, the three constitutional branches have structured agency rulemaking in a variety of other ways in recent years. One important development which has affected rulemaking, as well as the administrative process in general, has been the liberalization of standing criteria by the courts. Before the late 1960s, the ability to sue was restricted largely to parties who had suffered a direct material loss as the result of an agency's actions. In contrast, standing to seek judicial review has been expanded from the concept of legal rights protected under the common law to include statutorily protected interests. Thus, for example, the ostensible beneficiaries of regulatory policy have been afforded the opportunity to challenge administrative actions, even though their individual stakes in agency policy have been very small materially, or aesthetic or ideological in nature. Standing has further been extended in some instances to surrogate parties representing statutorily protected interests.[54] The liberalization of standing in these ways has enhanced the ability of individuals and groups, as well as judges, to influence agency decision making, especially in the new areas of health, safety, environmental, and consumer regulation. As Kenneth Warren observes:

The relaxation of standing requirements in the past decade or so has been largely responsible for a new flood of cases in such citizen-consumer areas as consumer, environmental, and housing law. This development is one of the chief reasons that administrative law has become so important in recent years to the study of public administration and public policy.[55]

Regulatory-enabling legislation enacted since the mid–1960s has also provided substantial opportunities for affected interests to participate in the rulemaking process. Statutes have typically included such features a mandatory consultation with advisory committees and other agencies, increased opportunities for judicial review of administrative decisions, and the provision of funds to aid those who wish to participate in or challenge agency proceedings. Although requirements such as consultation with advisory committees and other agencies have a long tradition in the American administrative process, dating well back into the nineteenth century, these devices were formerly much more common in "distributive" than in regulatory areas.[56] For instance, the regulatory statutes which created the ICC, the FTC, the SEC, and the FCC were devoid of reference to advisory committees. The probable explanation for this is that regulatory agencies were considered to be quasi-judicial, expert bodies whose objectivity might be impaired by outside influence. In contrast, opportunities for affected interests to intervene in decision making have expanded considerably under new regulatory legislation to the point where they often permeate the administrative process. Equally as important is the fact that these mechanisms have come more and more to present formal, legal opportunities for outside parties to shape agency rules.

Recent enabling statutes have provided opportunities for external actors to influence decisions throughout the administrative policy-making process. A good illustration of this is the Occupational Safety and Health Act of 1970, which created the OSHAdministration (within the Department of Labor) and vested it with broad powers to ensure safety in the workplace. Under this legislation, a preliminary rulemaking proceeding may be initiated on the basis of information provided by the Secretary of Labor, the Secretary of Health and Human Services, the National Institute for Occupational Safety and Health (NIOSH), a state or political subdivision thereof, or any "interested person." In practice, most rulemaking proceedings have begun with a recommendation by NIOSH, an organization within Health and Human Services created by the OSHAct to conduct research and advise OSHA.[57]

Once the potential need for a regulation has been established, OSHA is encouraged by its enabling legislation to appoint an *ad hoc* committee to formulate and recommend a safety standard. Such committees (which have usually been appointed) must represent the viewpoints of workers, employers, and state health and safety organizations. At least one of their members must be selected by the Secretary of Health and Human Services. The requirements that OSHA solicit written comment and hold oral hearings guarantee participation by outside parties during rulemaking proceedings.

One can cite many other agencies which have been required by their enabling legislation to allow input from numerous groups and other governmental entities. An extreme example was the Consumer Products Safety Commission (CPSC). Under the Consumer Products Safety Act of 1972, interested parties could petition the CPSC to initiate rulemaking proceedings. If the agency chose to deny such a petition, it had to state its reasons in the *Federal Register*. Furthermore, petitioners retained the right to bring action in district court to force the agency to initiate rulemaking. After a proceeding had begun, the Commission was required to solicit offers from outside parties to develop appropriate safety standards. The agency was bound to accept one of these submissions as a proposed rule, provided that at least one offerer proved to be "technically competent." In most cases, the CPSC could not interfere with an outside party's development of a standard, and could not concurrently develop a policy of its own. Following public hearings on a proposed rule and the adoption of a final standard, interested parties could again petition the agency to bring an enforcement proceeding against an alleged violator. In fact, actions could be brought against violators in federal court in the event of CPSC reluctance. These procedures proved to be so effective in guaranteeing participation that an overburdened CPSC persuaded Congress in 1981 to delete the petition and offerer requirements from its enabling legislation.[58]

The legislative provisions discussed above, as well as the expansion of standing by the courts, have structured agency discretion in such a way as to ensure that due consideration is given to relevant, often competing interests. In many cases, recent requirements have gone beyond the mere enhancement of opportunities to present arguments. Rather, they have increased the number of formal, authoritative participants in administrative decision making. Using a popular metaphor, the boundaries of administrative policy-making systems have been blurred or made more permeable, or have been expanded beyond agencies themselves to include elements of what is normally thought of as the environment, such as interest groups, other agencies, and the courts.

One should qualify these observations by noting that the Supreme Court seems to have retreated somewhat from its previous expansion of standing criteria in a few cases since the mid–1970s, and that Congress has terminated several programs designed to facilitate influence over agency decision making by outside groups. Perhaps enthusiasm for participation in the administrative process has begun to wane, as Martin Shapiro contends.[59] Such reversions have been isolated, however, and their significance should not be overdrawn. Most statutory provisions guaranteeing interest representation in agency rulemaking have remained intact, and the courts' posture on standing has continued to be liberal (if somewhat inconsistent) on the whole.[60] As a matter of perspective, whatever erosion has occurred along these lines remains slight compared with the advances that have taken place over the past two decades.[61]

The Use of Cost-Benefit Analysis

Another important development in the proces of regulatory rulemaking has been the increased use of cost-benefit analysis and related devices which emphasize the identification, quantification, and comparison of policy effects. Although the application of cost-benefit analysis is often complex, relying on expertise from a variety of fields, its basic premise is simple. Decision makers examine the probable effects of proposed actions to determine whether their total benefits to society will outweigh their total costs. In addition, benefit-to-cost ratios may be used to select the best policy from among several alternatives. Under a full or formal cost-benefit analysis, all policy effects are expressed in terms of real or imputed market values. With regard to the latter, a variety of techniques have been developed for assigning dollar equivalents to such things as human lives and a scenic environment. "Soft" values such as these may be treated qualitatively under less rigorous versions of cost-benefit analysis.[62]

Cost-benefit analysis came to prominence in the mid–1960s as a tool for evaluating Great Society programs, and its popularity has continued to grow since then. Since the mid–1970s, its use in the area of regulation has expanded dramatically. This has resulted from agency initiative, but has also been imposed or encouraged from without.

Several presidential directives have required executive agencies to weigh all or some of the positive and negative effects of regulatory proposals. "Inflationary impact analyses" and "regulatory analyses" were instituted by the Ford and Carter administrations, respectively, to provide information which agencies could use at their discretion in arriving at decisions. The most ambitious effort along these lines to date has been President Reagan's Executive Order 12291. It requires a comprehensive "regulatory impact analysis," which must quantify costs and benefits "to the maximum extent possible" for all "major regulations" proposed by executive branch agencies. What is presumably a less rigorous analysis is required for non-major rules.[63] The Reagan order also empowers the Office of Management and Budget to review agency studies and to delay and recommend disapproval of proposed actions found to be improperly justified. (The president's legal authority to disapprove regulations is a matter of controversy, but he can, of course, remove department heads.)

Cost-benefit analysis has also been encouraged by new regulatory statutes which require agencies to weigh and balance various competing policy objectives before issuing regulations. As a representative example, the Consumer Products Safety Act stipulates that safety rules reflect a consideration of the risks of injury, the number of products subject to the rule, the public need for the products, the probable effect of the rule on the utility, cost, and availability of the products, and means of minimizing adverse effects on competition and manufacturing. The Congressional Office of Technology Assessment has determined that similar balancing considerations are required under many of the provisions of the following laws:

Federal Insecticide, Fungicide, and Rodenticide Act

Federal Hazardous Substances Act

Consumer Products Safety Act

Toxic Substances Control Act

Federal Food, Drug, and Cosmetics Act

Occupational Safety and Health Act

Clean Water Act

Clean Air Act[64]

These statutes generally do not require formal cost-benefit analysis, or any other decisional methodology for that matter. As Michael Baram observes, however, agencies have felt increasing pressure from several sources to quantify the likely effects of proposed regulations under balancing mandates. Although judicial decisions have been inconsistent on the question of cost-benefit analysis in such instances, there has been a general tendency for the courts to require more rigorous justification for agency actions. In addition, the use of cost-benefit analysis has been widely advocated by economists, engineers, and scientists serving as agency consultants and as members of advisory committees. These pressures, coupled with growing public concern about the social and economic costs of regulation, have induced administrators to conduct full or limited cost-benefit analyses in many instances.[65] Generally applicable laws have required rigorous evaluation of policy effects as well. The most important of these is the Environmental Policy Act of 1969, which requires environmental-impact statements (EISs) for "all major federal actions affecting the quality of the human environment." An EIS must analyze the positive and negative effects of a proposed action on the environment and must also evaluate possible alternative policies. The Enviromental Policy Act does not mandate the quantification of policy effects (although it does encourage a "systematic, inter-disciplinary approach which will ensure the integrated use of the natural and social sciences"), but many agencies have seen fit to conduct fully or partially quantified analyses for the same general reasons discussed in the paragraph above.[66] Beyond current requirements, it appears as if the use of cost-benefit analysis in the area of regulation will continue to expand in the future. For example, the reform legislation alluded to earlier would have required a positive cost-benefit analysis as a justification for all major federal regulations.[67]

The rationale for cost-benefit analysis and related devices has been to structure and in a sense simplify decision making by "reducing relevant decisional factors to numbers that can be added, subtracted and compared."[68] Their popularity is largely due to the apparent sensibility of the premise that government policies should do more good than harm. Relatedly, such techniques are appealing because they force decision makers to consider all the likely consequences of their proposed actions. (Of course, bureaucrats have often been criticized for their commitments to narrow program goals at the expense of broader public interests.) Finally, the attractiveness of cost-benefit analysis and its kin can be attributed to their seeming objectivity and their enlistment of science in the pursuit of sound government policy. The process of tracing and measuring likely policy effects is based upon principles from economics, and in addition, often draws on expertise and data from other social sciences, engineering, and the hard sciences. On its face, at least, cost-benefit analysis is an instrumental technique for achieving the goal of "net welfare" or "economic efficiency." As two of its leading advocates state, for instance; "economists are neither the creators nor the dictators of values. They merely provide a procedure for inferring and pursuing existing values; their role is descriptive or "positive" rather than prescriptive or "normative."[69]

Expanding Congressional Control through the Legislative Veto

A final development in the area of rulemaking, which until recently appeared to be very significant, has been the attempt by Congress to gain more control over agency decisions through the legislative veto. Although mechanisms vary a good deal in their specifics, vetoes essentially require that agency regulations be submitted to Congress (or an element thereof) for review and approval before going into effect. Vetoes have existed since 1932, but were used largely to control individual application decisions before 1970. Since 1972, however, they have been applied to delegations of rulemaking authority in areas such as safety regulation by the Consumer Products Safety Commission, energy pricing by the Federal Energy Regulatory Commission, and the regulation of commercial practices by the Federal Trade Commission.[70]

Of course, one might argue that a discussion of the veto's growing popularity has been rendered mute in large part by the Supreme Court's 1983 *Chadha* decision. In this case involving congressional review of a decision by the Immigration and Naturalization Service, the Court seemingly declared the most popular forms of the veto unconstitutional. At the same time, however, it appears as if some forms of the veto will survive. Since the *Chadha* decision was based upon the presentation clause, two-house vetoes which require the president's signature should remain valid. Indeed, Congress appears to be eager to institute such mechanisms in order to maintain or extend its influence over agency rulemaking.[71]

CONCLUSION

As discussed in Chapter 2, the administrative process is the medium through which we attempt to mitigate the tension bureaucratic discretion presents for our political system. If we cannot avoid delegating policy-making authority to officials who are not directly accountable to the people, the next best thing is to structure their decision making. In this way we attempt to promote qualities we value in the process of agency decision making, *per se*, and to facilitate oversight of administration by the three constitutional branches of government.

If structural mechanisms serve as antidotes for the problems posed by administrative discretion, then one would expect their use to be a function of the magnitude of discretion itself. This has certainly been the case. It was not until 1946, after the New Deal, that Congress imposed broadly applicable requirements governing rulemaking and adjudication. Then, as the delegation of regulatory authority accelerated again in the 1960s and 1970s, Congress and the courts became dissatisfied with the Administrative Procedure Act as the only constraint on agency discretion. This was especially true in the area of rulemaking, where the APA's informal requirements provided no guarantee that agencies would consider relevant comments and which gave administrators wide latitude in justifying their decisions.

The fact that rulemaking has become more popular as a means of carrying out regulatory mandates has increased incentives for procedural reform. As discussed in the preceding chapter, the rulemaking revolution in the 1970s can be viewed in part as an effort to structure agency discretion. Thus, rulemaking has often been required or encouraged as a fairer, more comprehensive, and more forceful way of developing policy. But the increased use of rulemaking has also caused administration to have more immediate and widespread effects on society, and thus it has exacerbated the problems inherent in bureaucratic discretion. Indeed, this is a recurrent theme in Chapters 5 and 6, which are concerned in part with the repercussions of the Federal Trade Commission's increased reliance on rulemaking in recent years.

Administrative processes and procedures can be viewed, then, as means of mitigating the problems inherent in bureaucratic discretion by ensuring that agency decision making conforms with broad political and administrative norms. As discussed in the concluding chapter, this perspective lends important insights as to the reasons for and significance of administrative institutions. It does not, however, provide a fully sufficient basis for analysis, because the structural mechanisms which constrain agencies also reflect the influence of groups who wish to further their own interests. This was evident, for example, in the earlier discussion of the political pressures which helped shape the Administrative Procedure Act's rulemaking requirements. Conservative business interests favored trial-like procedures, such as those of the Walter-Logan Bill, which they felt would impede bureaucratic regulation. In contrast, liberals favored less-restrictive procedures which would facilitate administrative action. The liberals were ultimately successful in large part, but not without adding certain concessions to the APA.

As the following two chapters illustrate, normative considerations as well as group influences are useful in analyzing the political significance of administrative procedures in the Federal Trade Commission. The Commission's emphasis on rulemaking in recent years has been justified in part by the argument that such an approach serves the interests of good administration, yet it has also come at the behest of consumer representatives advocating more forceful regulation. Similarly, Congress' stipulation of hybrid procedures with a new grant of rulemaking authority for the FTC in 1974 was due in part to its misgivings about such a broad delegation and its desire to ensure that discretion would be exercised in an acceptable (and thus legitimate) manner. However, hybrid procedures also came as a concession to business groups who opposed FTC rulemaking, and who perceived that they could use due process requirements to delay and even prevent the issuance of unwanted regulations.

NOTES

1. For a discussion of the development of regulation in these and other areas see Theodore J. Lowi, *The End of Liberalism* (New York: W. W. Norton, 1969) pp. 128–46.

2. John P. Comer, *Legislative Functions of the National Administrative Authorities* (New York: Columbia University Press, 1927) p. 201.

3. These anti-bureaucratic sentiments were expressed passionately in several popular books of the period (as their titles clearly suggest). Gordon Hewart, *The New Despotism* (London: Ernest Benn, 1929); James M. Beck, *Our Wonderland of Bureaucracy* (New York: Macmillan Publishing Company, 1932); and Carleton K. Allen, *Bureaucracy Triumphant* (London: Oxford University Press, 1931).

4. Beck, *supra* note 3. Quoted from Kenneth Culp Davis, *Administrative Law and Government* (St. Paul, Minnesota: West Publishing Company, 1975) p. 12.

5. James Hart, "The Exercise of Rule-Making Power," *Report of the President's Committee on Administrative Management* (Washington, D.C.: U.S. Government Printing Office, 1937) p. 323.

6. *Ibid.*, pp. 323–24.

7. David A. Simmons before the House of Representatives Committee on the Judiciary, June 21, 1945. Quoted from *The Administrative Procedure Act: A Legislative History* (Washington, D.C.: U.S. Government Printing Office, 1946, Senate Doc. 248, 79th Cong., 2d. Sess.) p. 51.

8. For a discussion of the Walter-Logan Bill as it compared with the Administrative Procedure Act see Foster H. Sherwood, "The Federal Administrative Procedure Act," *American Political Science Review*, 41 (April, 1947).

9. *The Administrative Procedure Act, supra* note 7, p. 244.

10. *Ibid.*

11. Sherwood, *supra* note 8, p. 273.

12. *Ibid.*

13. See, for example, Sherwood, *supra* note 8; Frederick F. Blachly and Miriam E. Oatman, "Sabotage of the Administrative Process," *Public Administration Review*, 6 (1946); and Marver H. Bernstein, *Regulating Business by Independent Commission* (Princeton, New Jersey: Princeton University Press, 1955), especially chapter 7.

14. Sherwood, *supra* note 8, p. 275.

15. Blachly and Oatman, *supra* note 13, p. 226.

16. Davis, *supra* note 4; and James O. Freedman, *Crisis and Legitimacy: The Administrative Process and American Government* (Cambridge: Cambridge University Press, 1978) p. 8.

17. Bernstein, *supra* note 13, p. 194.

18. 60 Stat. 237 (1946), as amended. 5 U.S.C.A. secs. 551–559, 701–706, 1305, 3105, 3344, 5372, 7521. See sec. (a)(2)(C) for exceptions.

19. For a discussion, see Robert W. Hamilton, "Procedures for the Adoption of Rules of General Applicability: The Need for Procedural Innovation in Administrative Rulemaking," *California Law Review*, 60 (1972) pp. 1276–83.

20. In its report on the APA the Senate Judiciary Committee cited the report of the attorney general's committee approvingly:

> The Attorney General's Committee found that public rule making procedures "are likely to be diffused and of little real value either to the participating parties or the agency, unless their subject matter is indicated in advance.... In principle, therefore, each agency should be obliged to announce with the greatest possible definiteness the matters to be discussed in rule making proceedings."

The Administrative Procedure Act, supra note 7, p. 18.

21. As the Senate Judiciary Committee stated in its report, "Considerations of practicality, necessity, and public interest . . . will naturally govern the agency's determination of the extent to which public proceedings should go." *Ibid.*, pp. 200–1

22. *Ibid.*, pp. 20–21.

23. *Ibid.*, pp. 191 *et. seq.*

24. See Hamilton, *supra* note 19, for a discussion of formal procedures and where they are required.

25. Davis, *supra* note 4, p. 123.

26. *The Administrative Procedure Act, supra* note 7, p. 18.

27. *Ibid.*

28. See, for example, Arthur Bonfield, "Public Participation in Federal Rulemaking Relating to Public Property, Loans, Grants, Benefits, or Contracts," *University of Pennsylvania Law Review*, 119 (1970); and Roger Crampton, "The Why, Where, and How of Broadened Public Participation in the Administrative Process," *Georgetown Law Review*, 60 (1972).

29. *The Administrative Procedure Act, supra* note 7, 199.

30. For a discussion of this survey and its findings see Bonfield, *supra* note 28, and Bonfield, "Representing the Poor in Federal Rulemaking," *Michigan Law Review*, 67 (1969).

31. *Ibid.*

32. *Ibid.*

33. Kenneth Culp Davis, *Administrative Law Treatise* (St. Paul, Minnesota: West Publishing Company, 1958); and Davis, *Discretionary Justice* (Baton Rouge, Louisiana: Louisiana State University Press, 1969).

34. Barry Checkoway and Jon Van, "What Do We Know About Citizen Participation? A Selective Review of Research," in Stuart

Langton, ed., *Citizen Participation in America* (Lexington, Massachusetts: Lexington Books, 1978) p. 32.
    35. *Federal Register*, 36 (1971) p. 2532.
    36. Davis, *supra* note 33.
    37. Bonfield, "Representing the Poor," *supra* note 30.
    38. Crampton, *supra* note 28, p. 525.
    39. Bruce Frederickson *et al.*, *Facilitating Public Participation in Federal Agencies: Hearings Before the Subcommittee on Administrative Practices and Procedures of the Senate Judiciary Committee*, 94th Cong., 2d. Sess. (1976) pp. 483–85.
    40. William Pederson, "Formal Records and Informal Rulemaking," *Yale Law Journal*, 85 (1975) p. 51.
    41. A. Lee Fritschler, *Smoking and Politics* (Englewood Cliffs, New Jersey: Prentice-Hall, 1975) p. 90.
    42. Hamilton, *supra* note 19.
    43. Davis, *supra* note 4, pp. 121–25.
    44. *Ibid.*, p. 124.
    45. For a discussion of hybrid procedures imposed by Congress before 1972 see Hamilton, *supra* note 19.
    46. S. 1080, passed March 14, 1982.
    47. *Citizens to Preserve Overton Park v. Volpe*, 401 U.S. 402 (1971).
    48. *Vermont Yankee Nuclear Power Corp. v. Natural Resources Defense Council, Inc.*, 435 U.S. 519 (1978).
    49. Stephen DeLong, "Informal Rulemaking and the Integration of Law and Policy," *Virginia Law Review*, 65 (1979) p. 314.
    50. For a good discussion of recent developments in the area of *ex parte* communications see Paul R. Verkuil, "Jawboning Administrative Agencies: Ex Parte Contacts by the White House," *Columbia Law Review*, 80 (1980) pp. 971–78.
    51. *Ibid.*, p. 973.
    52. Consumer Products Safety Act, House Report No. 92–1153, p. 38.
    53. *Ibid.*, p. 973.
    54. For a thoughtful discussion of these developments see Richard B. Stewart, "The Reformation of American Administrative Law," *Harvard Law Review*, 88 (1975).
    55. Kenneth F. Warren, *Administrative Law in the American Political System* (St. Paul, Minnesota: West Publishing Company, 1982) p. 382.
    56. James Hart, *The Ordinance Making Power of the President of the United States* (Baltimore: John Hopkins University Press, 1925).
    57. Albert L. Nichols and Richard Zeckhauser, "Government Comes

to the Workplace: An Assessment of OSHA," *The Public Interest*, 49 (Fall, 1977).

58. The Omnibus Budget Reconciliation Act, passed August 13, 1981, made it less incumbent upon the CPSC to respond to petitioners and made the solicitation and acceptance of offers to develop standards optional. PL 97–35, 95 Stat. 718–20.

59. Martin Shapiro, "On Predicting the Future of Administrative Law," *Regulation Magazine* (July/August, 1979), pp. 26–34.

60. Warren, *supra* note 55, pp. 392–95.

61. One legislative program to wither away in recent years has been the FTC's intervenor funding, established in 1974 to aid consumer representatives and small businesses who could not otherwise afford to participate effectively in rulemaking proceedings. Other casualties have been the petition and offerer provisions pertaining to CPSC rulemaking discussed above in the text. The court case cited most frequently as a conservative precedent in the area of standing is *Warth v. Seldin*, 422 U.S. 490 (1975), which denied standing to a surrogate party. According to Warren (*supra* note 55), however, *Warth* has even "helped to encourage the lower courts to continue to liberalize standing law," due in part to its shaky five-to-four majority. Warren also observes that subsequent Supreme Court decisions have contradicted *Warth's* denial of standing to third parties.

62. The term "cost-benefit analysis" is often used loosely without qualification as to the specific methodology or extent of quantification required. For an extensive discussion of cost-benefit analysis and its use by federal regulatory agencies see Michael Baram, "Cost-Benefit Analysis: An Inadequate Basis for Health, Safety, and Environmental Regulatory Decisionmaking," *Ecology Law Quarterly*, 9 (1980). Also see Mark S. Thompson, *Benefit-Cost Analysis for Program Evaluation* (Beverly Hills: Sage Publications, 1980).

63. E.O. 12291 was promulgated on February 17, 1981. "Major regulations" are defined as those having an economic impact in excess of $100 million. The Office of Management and Budget is empowered to review agency determinations as to whether a regulation is major.

64. Baram, *supra* note 62, pp. 479–81.

65. *Ibid.*

66. *Ibid.*

67. S. 1080, *supra* note 46. As with the Reagan order, a major regulation is defined as one having an economic impact of more than $100 million.

68. Baram, *supra* note 62, p. 478.

69. Edith Stokey and Richard Zeckhauser, *A Primer for Policy Analysis* (New York: W. W. Norton, 1978) pp. 259–60.

70. Clark F. Norton, *Congressional Review, Deferral, and Disapproval of Executive Actions: A Summary and an Inventory of Statutory Authority*, Report 76–88 G (Washington, D.C.: Congressional Research Service, 1976), as supplemented by his reports 78–117 Gov. 25 May 1978, 79–47 Gov. 12 February 1979, and 82–26 Gov. 12 February 1982.

71. *Immigration and Naturalization Service v. Chadha, U.S. Law Week*, 51 (21 June 1983) pp. 4907–18. Another possible alternative would be to require rules to be *approved* by a joint resolution of Congress, which would then have to be signed by the president.

●5 Politics and Rulemaking in the Federal Trade Commission

The history of FTC rulemaking illustrates well the political significance of administrative processes and procedures. The issuance of Trade Regulation Rules (in lieu of adjudication) and the choice of procedures to guide rulemaking decisions have been perceived as having important substantive implications and, as a result, have been of considerable interest to those affected by FTC policy. Not surprisingly, therefore, decisions on these matters by the agency and by Congress have been influenced by the Commission's political environment as well as by considerations of good administration. In turn, the choice among alternative processes and procedures has helped shape the FTC's policy and has ultimately had a profound effect on the agency's political fortunes as well.

This chapter examines FTC rulemaking up through the passage of the Magnuson-Moss Act in 1974, focusing primarily on the determinants of institutional choice. Magnuson-Moss is a logical breaking point, for it signaled a new era in FTC rulemaking in two respects. The act cleared up doubts concerning the legality of Trade Regulation Rules that had always impeded the agency's efforts, and it generally seemed to encourage FTC rulemaking as a more effective means of consumer protection. Yet Magnuson-Moss also imposed rulemaking procedures much more burdensome than the informal ones the Commission had been using. Chapter 6 discusses the implications of the FTC's heightened rulemaking activity subsequent to Magnuson-Moss, as well as the effects of its new rulemaking procedures.

INTRODUCTION

In 1914 Congress, which was struggling with the problem of trusts, passed the Clayton and Federal Trade Commission acts. The latter statute created the Federal Trade Commission and gave it the mission of policing "unfair practices" in commerce. This vague mandate was generally intended to enable the Commission to deal with unethical actions undertaken by one firm which adversely affected another firm or firms. The most prominent type of monopolizing behavior that Congress was trying to prevent was a large firm attempting to run a smaller competitor out of business by undercutting prices.

The FTC was also empowered to confront deception, such as misleading, exaggerated, or false claims concerning a product's characteristics or performance. Under its original charter, however, the agency was authorized to prevent only that deception which had an adverse effect on other businesses—that is, deception which constituted an unfair competitive practice. Deception which merely harmed consumers technically lay outside the FTC's mandate. Although the Commission sometimes ignored or attempted to circumvent this distinction in its first years, a Supreme Court decision in 1923 explicitly confined the agency's authority to instances in which unfair practices affected a business competitor.[1] Consumer protection, therefore, could only be incidental to actions undertaken for another purpose. The Commission's mandate remained unchanged until 1938, when Congress passed the Wheeler-Lea Act, empowering the FTC to prevent deception for the purpose of consumer protection.

Today, competitive practices and consume protection remain the FTC's two primary areas of concern. The Commission issues rules to prevent unfairness and deception in furtherance of both these ends, although consumer protection is by far the more commonly stated basis for rulemaking. With one exception, the FTC has not used rulemaking as a means of antitrust enforcement concerning issues other than deception, such as illegal mergers and anti-competitive pricing.[2] One of the agency's rationales for not issuing rules in these latter areas has been that individual violations are often unique in character and should therefore be dealt with on a case-by-case basis. In contrast, deceptive practices often occur on an industry-wide basis. Several statutes of limited scope, such as the Fur Products Labeling Act of 1945, have given the Commission explicit but circumscribed power to issue rules regulating particular industries. The concern here, however, is with rulemaking pursuant to the agency's principal enabling legislation, the FTC Act, which gives the Commission authority to police commerce in general.

THE DETERMINANTS OF FTC RULEMAKING

The Controversial Adoption of Rulemaking Authority

The FTC did not begin issuing substantive rules until 1962. Until then it had relied primarily on case-by-case adjudication in attempting to protect consumers and industry from deception in the marketplace. Adjudications were sometimes precipitated by complaints submitted to the Commission, and sometimes resulted from the agency's own investigations. Formal, trial-like hearings would be held for the purposes of determining (1) whether or not the party in question did, indeed, engage in the alleged practice, and (2) whether or not that practice was unfair or deceptive. In a 1979 report to Congress, the Commission described its role under adjudication as that of a law enforcement agency implying that its task was merely to ensure compliance with the FTC Act.[3] In truth, of course, the Commission was making policy in a very real sense by defining what was unfair or deceptive through precedent.

Although adjudication was the only tool the FTC used which had legal, coercive force, the Commission employed a variety of other, informal techniques to police deception. The agency began issuing Trade Practice Rules (TPRs) in 1919. These were limited in their effects to particular industries, and were drawn up with the help of industry representatives in "trade practice conferences." Proceedings of this kind were sometimes initiated by the Commission, but often came at the request of trade associations who wished to establish codes of fair play for their members. In 1955 the FTC also began issuing Guides. These were designed to perform the educational function of spelling out in detail the requirements of laws administered by the Commission. While most Guides were applicable to specific industries, some pertained to all commercial activity.

TPRs and Guides were interpretive rules (see Chapter 3). As such, they served to refine the meaning of "unfair or deceptive" in particular areas, but had no legal force. Since compliance with their terms was voluntary, their main function was to warn industry of what the FTC might consider grounds for adjudicatory action in the future. The crucial determination of whether or not the practices described in TPRs and Guides were unfair or deceptive still had to be substantiated in adjudicatory proceedings against individual violators.

Aside from TPRs and Guides, the Commission also used advisory opinions and consent orders as informal means of preventing deception. As statements of how the agency might view the legality of proposed actions, advisory opinions were usually given to potentially affected industry members upon request. Consent orders were voluntary agreements between the Commission and a party about to enter, or in the course of, adjudicatory proceedings.[4] Naturally, the usefulness of consent orders depended upon the willingness of accused parties to reach agreement with the FTC, or perhaps more accurately, their disinclination to go through adjudicatory proceedings.

The Commission still uses the devices discussed above. In 1962, however, it added supplementary or "substantive" rules to its consumer-protection arsenal. The agency referred to these as Trade Regulation Rules. The decision to begin issuing TRRs was anomalous in that the Federal Trade Commission Act said nothing explicitly indicating that the FTC could issue rules which had the force and effect of law. The Commission's apparent lack of rulemaking power was reinforced by precedent, since the FTC had considered itself strictly an adjudicatory agency for almost fifty years. As one might expect, the decision was very controversial.[5]

The Commission later defended its adoption of rulemaking

as legally justifiable on several grounds. One was that such authority was implicit in its mandate to *prevent* unfair or deceptive practices. The FTC noted that adjudication was inadequate for this purpose because it had only remedial effect. The Commission also maintained that TRRs were neither legislative nor interpretive. Rather, they were substantive, just as judge-made common law.[6] The agency's reasoning here was that if it had the power to make what were, *in effect*, rules in the course of adjudication, it also had the power to use rulemaking procedure for the same purpose. The FTC attempted to strengthen this argument by pointing to several Supreme Court decisions affirming agency discretion in the choice of administrative procedure. A final point made by the Commission was that although rulemaking was not authorized in Section 5 of the FTC Act (which conferred the power to prevent unfair or deceptive practices), it was authorized in Section 6(g), which said that the Commission could "make rules and regulations for the purpose of carrying out the provisions of this Act."[7]

Those opposed to the FTC's assumption of rulemaking power contended in subsequent proceedings before the agency, Congress, and the courts that the Commission could not issue TRRs without an explicit grant of authority to do so. They argued that Section 6(g) of the FTC Act was intended only to authorize rules of internal practice and procedure, and that nothing in the language of the statute hinted that its framers had meant the FTC to issue substantive rules.[8] Moreover, opponents argued that Congress certainly would have been explicit if it had intended to delegate such an important power to the Commission. Instead, they pointed to evidence in the FTC Act's legislative history which indicated that at least some congressmen did not want the Commission to issue rules. For example, one Conference Committee member had stated that "the Federal Trade Commission will have no power to prescribe the methods of competition to be used in the future. In issuing its orders it will not be exercising power of a legislative nature."[9]

The Increased Attractiveness of Rulemaking

In view of the questionable legal basis of TRRs, it is understandable that the Commission's decision to adopt rulemaking

was not an easy one. In 1961, Commissioner Everette Mac-
Intyre, the FTC's foremost proponent of rulemaking, stated
publicly that the Commission was empowered to issue substantive rules having the force and effect of law. Later, however, he retreated, stating before the Miami-Dade Chamber of
Commerce that a TRR would only establish a *prima facie* case,
and that a respondent could show that a rule should not be
regarded as legally binding during an adjudication.[10] Likewise,
FTC chairman Paul Dixon stated that rules which had "the
force and effect of law" were authorized by Section 6(g) of the
FTC Act, but later said that the Commission had no intention
of issuing substantive rules and that TRRs "would not be law
in any sense."[11] Given the thorny nature of the issue, coupled
with the conventional wisdom that established agencies are
docile beasts guided by inertia, what explains the FTC's
decision?

The agency may have been influenced by considerations of
fairness such as those discussed in Chapter 3. These certainly
had a prominent place in the justifications it gave for rulemaking. Rather than arbitrarily singling out individuals from
groups of several or many violators, TRRs would treat entire
industries equitably. Moreover, rules would have only future
effect; therefore, firms would not be punished for their failure
to predict what the Commission would define as unfair or deceptive. By the same token, TRRs would let potentially affected
parties plan their future actions more effectively, since they
would not have to wait for a series of precedent-establishing
decisions to discover what was illegal. Finally, rulemaking proceedings themselves were advocated as a better policy-making
device. Adjudication solicited only the views of the immediate
parties to a case, while rulemaking could consider comments
from the entire spectrum of affected interests.[12]

A more important reason for the FTC's adoption of rulemaking, however, was that TRRs represented an expedient and
effective way for the agency to pursue its policy goals in several
respects. The Commission was becoming increasingly frustrated with adjudication as its only legally binding enforcement
tool. Deceptive practices would often be widespread throughout
an industry, yet the FTC could attack only one violator at a

time. Others engaged in the same or similar practices could go on doing so until the Commission moved against them. Thus, it might take years to police an entire industry.

A related shortcoming of adjudication was that it had limited substantive scope, since the Commission could proscribe only those specific actions named in a suit. Restricted only by their imaginations, businesses were free to adopt new deceptive practices which were often similar to and had substantially the same effect as the ones proscribed in orders. As a leading student of the FTC has observed, firms can and do change their advertising messages and emphasis with great frequency. By the time a complaint—or even an application for a preliminary injunction—is entered, the firm has abandoned the questionable claims and made many others."[13]

A. Lee Fritschler's discussion of the FTC's frustration in attempting to regulate cigarette advertising attests to the ineffectiveness of adjudication as a means of preventing deception.

One of the early cases involving cigarette advertising points up the difficulties in commission procedures. The manufacturers of a now extinct brand called Julep cigarettes claimed in their advertisements that their product was a remedy for coughs. Even in the early 1940s this strained the credulity of the commission, and the Julep makers were forced to stop making the claim. Yet within a short period, other manufacturers advertised similar health claims. One producer claimed that there was not a cough in a carload of his cigarettes. The same manufacturer later announced that more doctors smoked his cigarette than any other brand.[14]

As Fritschler has characterized the FTC's thirty year of attempting to police the cigarette industry through adjudication, "The Commission found itself putting out brush fires of deception while the inferno raged on."[15]

Trade Practice Rules and Guides originally had been envisioned by the FTC as means of overcoming the problems posed by a purely adjudicatory approach. As generally applicable statements, they would pertain to all members of an industry, or more broadly, to all those engaged in a particular class of behavior. Also, they could be stated in sufficiently abstract terms, or with sufficient enumeration, to confront a group of

similar deceptive practices, possibly anticipating future industry inventiveness. As mere interpretive rules, however, TPRs
and Guides relied on voluntary compliance, and the Commission had become thoroughly disillusioned with their effectiveness by the 1960s. As Commissioner MacIntyre stated in 1961,
"The sad fact of the matter is that in a number of very important
areas, industry practices adverse to the trade generally, and
apparently inconsistent with the law, have been continued despite the advice set forth in Trade Practice Conference Rules
and Guides."[16]

The Commission came to view rulemaking, therefore, as a
much more effective policy-making tool for some areas. As with
TPRs and Guides, Trade Regulation Rules were general statements of policy which could apply to an entire industry or all
of commerce, and which could be expressed in such a way as
to anticipate variations on deceptive themes. But unlike these
interpretive rules, TRRs were legally binding. Once promulgated, they could be used as bases for adjudicatory actions
against parties who violated their terms. The essential advantage of this was that the Commission would only have to show
in subsequent adjudicatory proceedings that those accused had
violated the terms of TRRs and would not have to prove that
the acts themselves were unfair or deceptive. It was hoped that
TRRs would not only make adjudicatory proceedings easier,
but that they would also deter industry members from testing
the Commission as would likely be the case were the same
practices merely to be proscribed in TPRs or Guides.

Political Support for Rulemaking

Although the perception that TRRs would be a fairer and
more effective means of regulation was central to the Commission's adoption of rulemaking authority, this in itself is not
a fully sufficient explanation for the agency's action. FTC officials as well as other government influentials and scholars have
been aware of the potential advantages of rulemaking for years.
For example, the Brownlow Commission advocated that the
FTC issue rules as early as 1937.[17] Yet despite the apparent

utility of rulemaking, the Commission waited for almost half a century to issue its first TRR.

An important part of the explanation for the FTC's adoption of rulemaking is that policy demands on the agency had built to such an extent that it was forced to go beyond adjudication to retain some degree of effectiveness. Commerce in 1914 was vastly different from what it had become in the early 1960s. Not only had the number of products on the market increased dramatically with advancing technology, but so had their complexity. In a wide variety of industries, manufacturers had adopted the strategy that the best way to gain a larger share of the market was to incorporate extra conveniences or additives. For example, refrigerators in the 1940s and early 1950s had two operational units, but by 1970 the simplest model had at least seven and the most complex had sixty-three.[18] Of course, this technological trend was accompanied by great advances in the extent and sophistication of advertising. As "new," and "improved" became Madison Avenue watchwords, the variety of ways in which consumers could be misled or cheated multiplied.

Concomitant with these developments in the commercial sector, it is generally agreed that consumer awareness and activism began to take off in the late 1950s and early 1960s. Alan Stone has attributed this to two basic phenomena. First, the developments discussed above obviously created more reasons for consumers to be concerned. Second, the enormous expansion of higher education, coupled with a similar growth in public and quasi-public employment, created a new class of relatively sophisticated and articulate people who were free from the control and influence of the commercial sector.[19] Influential books such as John Kenneth Galbraith's *American Capitalism* and Vance Packard's *The Hidden Persuaders*, congressional hearings on monopoly power and administered prices, and extensive publicity from such events as the Food and Drug Administration's cranberry decision and the thalidomide controversy were both symptomatic and causative of the rise in consumerism.[20] Given this growing awareness, elected officials such as senators Warren Magnuson and Estes Kefauver began to realize the advantages of consumer advocacy. Politically, the consumer movement may have fully come to life with President Kennedy's proposal of a consumer's bill of rights in 1961.[21]

An agency's strength and survival typically depend upon its ability to maintain a favorable balance of political support. For most of its history, the only groups which were closely attuned to the FTC's activities were the industries it regulated, and the business community perceived that rulemaking, as a more forceful and expedient means of regulation, would have an adverse effect on its interests. (The nature and strength of industry's feelings on this subject will be treated in more detail later in this chapter.) The rise of consumerism gave the agency a viable alternative source of political support which enabled it to take a more aggressive regulatory stance.

Although direct consumer advocacy of FTC rulemaking, *per se*, is difficult to document, there is tangible evidence of such support in Congress. In 1957 the House Interstate and Foreign Commerce Committee established a subcommittee on legislative oversight which looked extensively into the performance of the independent commissions. According to Representative John Moss, who served on the subcommittee from 1958 to 1968, the FTC was subject to a good deal of adverse comment for its lack of diligence in the consumer protection area. None of the subcommittee's reports explicitly recommended rulemaking, yet it is safe to assume that a good deal of informal encouragement was given to the Commission. As Moss stated in regard to rulemaking, the subcommittee invited the Commission to stop being so timid and to go out and undertake to test the full reach of its powers . . . and to let the courts tell them when they had exceeded it rather than attempting beforehand to tightly circumscribe their own authority." He added that this was virtually a unanimous sentiment among the subcommittee.[22]

The Commission's Early TRRs

In 1962 the Commission announced its intention to promulgate Trade Regulation Rules.[23] Since the regulatory nature of TRRs clearly placed them under the ambit of the Administrative Procedure Act, the rules of practice adopted by the FTC satisfied the requirements of informal rulemaking. In addition, the FTC sought to legitimate its adoption of rulemaking by providing more-extensive opportunities to participate than the minimum requirements prescribed in Section 553. The Commission stated that it would hold hearings at its discretion, and in practice nearly all of its subsequent proceedings provided an opportunity for both oral and written comment. The rules of practice also provided that a tentative rule would be published in the *Federal Register* after the Commission had received comment pursuant to its initial notice of proposed rulemaking. Written comment concerning the tentative rule would be solicited before the agency made a final decision.

The FTC began issuing rules in an atmosphere of uncertainty. Although the Commission knew that it had some political support for rulemaking, it did not know how much. Because of this, and because of the questionable legality of TRRs, the agency's first rules were no more than token efforts to test the water. For example, the very first TRR stipulated that sleeping bag labels and advertisements must reflect the size of the finished product rather than that of the presewn material. Presewn measurements obviously overstated the size of sleeping bags, and were therefore deceptive. There was nothing controversial about such a rule, and the sleeping bag industry had little room for complaint. Most other early TRRs dealt with matters of equally low consequence and controversy, such as deception in advertising the size of table cloths. Guides would have probably been equally as effective for treating such issues, since the Commission would have had to spend little effort proving that the practices in question were deceptive and thus in violation of the FTC Act. In all likelihood, the purpose of these TRRs was to establish precedent for the exercise of rulemaking authority.

The Commission's first rulemaking effort of major consequence was its ill-fated requirement that health warnings be placed on cigarette packages. The cigarette rule was perceived to have adverse effects on a powerful industry and, in addition, raised several controversial issues. Tobacco interests challenged the Commission's factual assertions during notice-and-comment proceedings, introducing statistical evidence and expert testimony which contradicted the recently issued surgeon general's report on the health hazards of smoking (made public in January of 1964). They also argued that regardless of the possible ill effects of smoking, there was nothing inherently unfair or deceptive about the failure of manufacturers to discuss the dangers of cigarettes. This sort of remedial policy, they felt, went beyond the FTC's mandate. Finally, industry groups objected to the Commission's use of rulemaking itself as something that was not authorized by law.[24]

Undeterred by these objections, the Commission promulgated its cigarette rule in July, 1964. Resistance by tobacco interests and their supporters in Congress was so formidable, however, that a statute was soon enacted which nullified the TRR, imposing considerably less stringent disclosure requirements. Congress's lack of support "burned" the Commission, and as a result, the agency reverted to the issuance of trivial rules.[25] One of the most inane was a TRR specifying that advertisements for extension ladders must reflect the true length of the ladders, and not the length of the two halves (which of course overlap).

A More Aggressive Rulemaking Approach

The scope and effect of TRRs remained modest until the late 1960s. Then the Commission encountered a wave of criticism which changed its course. In 1969 a group of law students working for Ralph Nader compiled a report on the FTC which was highly critical of the agency's passiveness in the area of consumer protection.[26] Largely because of this report (which received considerable attention), President Nixon asked the American Bar Association to evaluate the Commission and to recommend ways in which its structure and activities could be improved. The ABA was also critical, and one of its primary recommendations was that the FTC rely more heavily on rulemaking as a more powerful consumer protection tool.[27] Shortly thereafter, Miles Kirkpatrick, who had headed the ABA study, was appointed by Nixon as FTC chairman.

Criticism of the Commission and the publicity surrounding

it spurred both popular and governmental support for FTC activism in the area of consumer protection. As a result, TRRs issued in the late 1960s and early 1970s were clearly more ambitious than their predecessors had been. They embraced more significant industry practices and relied on more controversial interpretations of the meaning of "unfair or deceptive." Some of the more notable FTC policy initiatives during this era were TRRs regulating the care labeling of textile wearing apparel, retail food store advertising, and the use of negative option plans by sellers in commerce, as well as a rule establishing a three-day cooling-off period for door-to-door sales.

In assessing the Commission's new emphasis on rulemaking, one authority observes that while pre–1969 rules tended to codify either agency policy that had already been established through adjudication or widely accepted norms of industry behavior, later rules tended to be purely legislative, having little basis in previously made FTC law.[28] Also, rules began to take on more of a prescriptive aspect in addition to proscribing behavior. For example, the Commission's octane rule required gasoline retailers to post octane ratings on their pumps and specified the measurement techniques through which these figures were to be derived.[29] Prior to 1969, prescriptive rules had been confined mainly to matters involving potential health hazards.

In contrast to most earlier rules, some of the FTC's new TRRs imposed significant economic costs on regulatees. Not surprisingly, therefore, the agency's vigor brought about considerable resistance from industry. Opposition was focused this time through the courts. In 1968 a federal district court denied a claim for injunctive relief, partially on the theory that the FTC lacked statutory authority to promulgate substantive rules. The D.C. Circuit Court avoided this issue on appeal, adding to the uncertainty regarding the legal status of TRRs.[30] Later, in 1971, the National Petroleum Refiners' Association successfully challenged the octane rule in district court, again on the grounds that the Commission did not possess rulemaking authority. This decision was eventually reversed at the circuit level in 1973, but during the interim the FTC's rulemaking activity almost came to a halt.[31]

The FTC Receives an Explicit Grant of Rulemaking Authority

As uncertainty and controversy persisted in the late 1960s and early 1970s concerning the legal status of TRRs, the Commission asked Congress to amend the FTC Act by providing an explicit grant of rulemaking power. Beginning in 1970, a series of bills were introduced proposing such an amendment. The history of this legislation clearly illustrates the significance attributed to rulemaking by members of the FTC's political environment.

Largely in response to the Nader report and the American Bar Association study which corroborated its findings, President Nixon called in October, 1969, for a revitalization of the FTC. Senators Magnuson, Baker, Griffin, Prouty, and Scott introduced the Consumer Protection Act of 1969 (S. 3201) for the administration on December 3 of that year. As introduced, S. 3201 contained nothing with regard to rulemaking. It proposed an expansion of the powers of the FTC from matters "in" commerce to those "in and affecting" commerce. It also provided for preliminary injunction authority and for the bringing of class actions in federal court based on final cease and desist orders issued by the Commission.[32] The Senate Commerce Committee called for hearings on S. 3201 later in December. The committee's majority sought to build support for the legislation by inviting testimony from FTC officials, as well as from various consumer representatives. An important product of these hearings was the contribution of additional ideas for reforming the FTC, among them an explicit grant of rulemaking authority. With the unanimous backing of the Commission, new FTC chairman Caspar Weinberger formally asked Congress to add rulemaking authority to the agency's enabling legislation in February of 1970. A committee print of S. 3201 prepared in May of 1970 was the first of a series of bills proposing a grant of rulemaking authority.

A wide array of industry groups, including such broadly representative organizations as the Chamber of Commerce of the United States and the National Association of Manufacturers, objected vehemently to the proposed delegation of rulemaking power to the FTC. They argued that such an open delegation by Congress in an area so expansive as interstate commerce was probably unconstitutional and certainly undesirable. Delegations of rulemaking authority to other agencies were confined to areas affecting single industries and usually limited administrative discretion to the pursuit of more concretely defined goals. In contrast, a statute permitting the FTC to make rules to prevent "unfair or deceptive practices in or affecting commerce" was criticized by industry as a delegation of the vaguest, broadest kind. Opponents of FTC rulemaking further claimed that TRRs were too inflexible to deal effectively with rapidly changing commercial practices. Relatedly, they argued that rulemaking was a crude device because it was insensitive to varying contextual factors. In these respects, industry groups maintained that an adjudicatory approach allowed FTC policy to "breathe" with society in the same way as common law.[33]

Opposition to the FTC's use of rulemaking was sometimes voiced in strong ideological terms. For instance, a congressman who was sympathetic to business interests stated:

Would you agree that the consumer in the United States has benefited to a greater degree in the availability of a variety of products at a fairer price to him under the system we have than anywhere else in the world.... It seems to me that the working of the market place itself is our best opportunity to see that the inefficient, that the manufacturer of shabby merchandise is eliminated from the market place.[34]

One group spokesman even went so far as to predict that a grant of such far-reaching rulemaking authority to unaccountable and overzealous bureaucrats would be tantamount to an "economic death sentence" for American industry.[35]

On the other hand, advocates of aggressive regulation contended that rulemaking authority was necessary if the FTC was to transcend its role as the "little old lady of Pennsylvania Avenue" and effectively protect consumers. Rulemaking would allow the Commission to establish broadly applicable standards more quickly and more economically. In addition, it was argued that rulemaking permitted more flexible and qualitatively broader policy making. For example, a former FTC staff attorney testified before the House Interstate and Foreign Commerce Committee that the innovative policy specifying that gasoline octane ratings be derived by averaging the results of the two currently popular measuring techniques probably could not have been established through adjudication. He argued that this would have been unfortunate, since the averaging systematically canceled out error inherent in each of the individual methods.[36]

Supporters of FTC rulemaking were able to marshal a good deal of learned opinion to back their arguments. As discussed in the preceding chapter, several respected judges, as well as numerous other scholars, had levied general criticisms against the use of adjudication for making broad policy. In addition, the Ash Council had recently recommended that regulatory agencies rely less on the case-by-case method and more on rulemaking, and the Administrative Conference of the United States had adopted a resolution specifically advocating the use of rulemaking by the Commission.[37]

Conflict over the FTC's authority was finally resolved in December, 1974, when Congress passed the Magnuson-Moss Warranty–Federal Trade Commission Improvement Act.[38] Along with the provision of significant new powers to regulate warranties, this legislation explicitly authorized the Commission to promulgate TRRs. Moreover, it sought to aid in the development of rules through an intervenor funding program, whereby the Commission could help defray the expenses of consumer representatives and others who could not otherwise afford to participate effectively in rulemaking proceedings. Magnuson-Moss reflected a strong pro-consumer mood in Congress and was intended not only to authorize but to encourage rulemaking.

PROCEDURAL REQUIREMENTS TO ACCOMPANY FTC RULEMAKING

If Magnuson-Moss seemed a victory for the FTC and consumer advocates, however, it was not without important concessions to the business community. The following discussion will take a closer look at the legislative history of Magnuson-Moss, focusing in some detail on Congress's selection of procedures to accompany the Commission's new grant of rulemaking authority. This issue was of considerable strategic importance to the FTC and members of its environment, who perceived that procedural choice would ultimately have important substantive policy effects. It was also important to congressmen who had simply developed misgivings about such a broad delegation of legislative power. The final version of Magnuson-Moss contained rulemaking procedures far more stringent than the informal ones the FTC had been using. The act may actually have been a victory for anti-regulation interests in this sense, given the fact that the FTC's authority to issue TRRs had been approved by the D.C. Circuit Court in 1973.

Procedures as a Political Issue

As discussed, the Consumer Protection Act of 1969 was revised in May of 1970 at the behest of the FTC to include a grant of rulemaking authority. In addition, the redraft of S. 3201 stipulated procedural requirements for FTC rulemaking which deviated from those of the APA (and those that the Commission had been using) in several important respects. The Commission would have to hold oral hearings *if requested.* These would be conducted in an informal manner, except that cross-examination would be allowed where the agency felt it "appropriate." In order to prevent redundant cross-examination, the FTC could group together participants with the same or similar interests. Another important feature of the redraft was the requirement that the Commission keep a rulemaking record composed of its hearing transcript and all written submissions. In promulgating a final rule, the agency would have to base its decision on the "relevant matter" contained in the record.[39]

The rulemaking procedures of S. 3201 were conceived by Lynn Sutcliffe, a young staff attorney for the Senate Commerce Committee. The issues of rulemaking and rulemaking procedure had not yet come to dominate the debate over FTC improvement legislation as they would in subsequent congresses. This was probably due to the fact that the business community had not had time to react to these newly posed issues. Nevertheless, Sutcliffe, who along with staff counsel Michael Pertschuk had responsibility for redrafting S. 3201, saw the potential for industry resistance to informal rulemaking procedures and recognized the need for compromise.[40] Considering the variety of formats proposed in subsequent bills, it is remarkable how closely the procedural requirements of S. 3201 resembled those finally passed in the Magnuson-Moss Act.

S. 3201 failed to receive floor action, and its counterpart, H.R. 14931, was not reported out of the House Interstate and Foreign Commerce Committee. In the Ninety-second Congress, the FTC-related provisions of S. 3201 were combined with warranty legislation that had been passed in the Senate in 1970, but that had not been acted upon by the House. This legislation (S. 986) was the first of a series of similar proposals considered by both houses which eventually culminated in the passage of the Magnuson-Moss Act in the Ninety-third Congress. Each of these bills had basically the same format. Title I consisted of warranty requirements, while Title II proposed measures designed to improve the performance of the FTC.

Initially, debate during hearings on FTC improvement legislation revolved around the advisability of rulemaking itself. As hearings progressed, however, it became increasingly apparent that Congress was determined to give the FTC permission to issue TRRs and that the courts might well uphold the agency's assumption of rulemaking authority at any rate. Opponents of FTC regulation made a pragmatic change in strategy, therefore, turning much of their attention to the procedures the Commission would be required to use in carrying out its legislative power.

The business community was unanimous in its opposition to the simple notice-and-comment rulemaking procedure advocated by the FTC and consumer groups. It was one thing, they argued, for elected representatives to make policy in an informal, legislative manner, but quite another for bureaucrats to do so. Industry groups thus urged Congress to constrain the FTC's discretion by imposing the APA's formal procedures. As discussed in Chapter 4, such a requirement would have imposed the same elements of due process on FTC rulemaking as required for adjudication. Industry spokesmen argued that the factual premises upon which the Commission based its decisions should be subject to cross-examination to ensure their validity. Relatedly, the requirement that final rules be based on a tested record would enable the courts to ensure the soundness of agency decisions. The following statements by representatives of the American Canners Association, the U.S. Chamber of Commerce, and the National Association of Manufacturers, respectively, illustrate the feelings of the business community in these regards:

In the typical trade regulation so-called hearing, anybody can come in and make an unsworn speech, present any wild assertion of fact, or submit a written statement that is never subject to answer or checking. Typically, the Commission can shovel into the so-called record generalizations and opinions based on unresolved and necessarily unverified fact.[41]

To assure the integrity of the decision-making process the decision maker should be required to consider the facts, to expose those facts to the crucible of cross-examination, and to be held to a decision based upon the weight of the evidence and logic. No such procedure is required or suggested here.[42]

I don't know what basis the court could use for evaluating whatever is in the four corners of the record as substantial or not. Suppose letters come in—let's say crank letters come in, and if you had the authors on the stand, your cross-examination would be able to show how ill-informed their comments and criticisms are. But you can't do that. How can any court look at one or more of those letters and say these are not substantial?[43]

The FTC and consumer advocates were just as adamant in their opposition to formal rulemaking as the business community was in its resistance to informal procedures. The Commission argued that simple notice and comment, as already practiced, was sufficient for gathering opinions and testing factual assertions. Formal due process guarantees were useful in a judicial setting, since jurors were inexperienced triers of fact. Most FTC administrators had legal training, however, and did not need such an aid.[44] In addition, the FTC and its supporters echoed the viewpoint popular among students of administrative law that formal procedures were inappropriate for dealing with policy questions and issues of legislative fact. In this regard, the Commission argued that the questions of fact it dealt with typically differed from those found in a judicial setting. Jurors had to determine if the defendant "did it," whereas FTC rules were typically based on much broader, probabilistic judgments.[45]

Perhaps the most telling argument made by the FTC was that formal procedures would be a great source of delay. Agency personnel and consumer representatives felt that regulated interests would stall the promulgation of needed rules for months and even years by exploiting their procedural rights and their ability to create an extensive record. As Commissioner Kirkpatrick stated:

In my opinion the Commission can adopt fair rules without the delays, the unending delays and interruptions I am fearful would really break down our rulemaking proceeding were full cross-examination and discovery as a matter of due process to be compulsory. I would be very apprehensive that it would be a month of Sundays and much longer before we could adopt a rule that was going to be unpopular to those who would be governed by it, and by and large, rules are not the most popular thing. People have to change their ways because of the existence of a rule, and the longer they can fend it off, the happier they are. That is my problem.[46]

The commission could point to delay—often extreme—that had apparently resulted from the use of formal procedures by other agencies.

Reaching a Compromise: The Dynamics of Procedural Choice

These arguments concerning the virtues and defects of formal and informal procedure were repeated often during the struggle over FTC improvement legislation. As mentioned, the Commerce Committee's redraft of S. 3201 in the Ninety-first Congress anticipated conflict of this sort, and contained compromise hybrid procedures which combined elements of the two

formats. Perhaps owing to the impetus of S. 3201, bills in subsequent Congresses proposed a variety of procedures designed
to strike a balance that would satisfy opponents and proponents
of FTC regulation.

In the Ninety-second Congress, S. 986 (introduced on February 25, 1971) contained FTC improvement features similar
to those of S. 3201. However, the bill's procedural requirements with respect to rulemaking differed somewhat from those
of its predecessor. As introduced, S. 986 would have required
the FTC to use informal procedures with certain modifications.
The Commission would hold oral hearings if requested, but
there was no mention of cross-examination. As in S. 3201, the
FTC would also be required to keep a rulemaking record, and
its final rules would have to be based on the substantial evidence therein.

Hearings on S. 986 were markedly different from those on
S. 3201. Whereas numerous consumer advocates had appeared
before Congress in response to S. 3201, hearings on S. 986 were
dominated by industry witnesses. Only Virginia Knauer of the
White House Office of Consumer Affairs testified in support of
the legislation, and even she, as an emissary of the conservative
Nixon administration, was equivocal in her support of FTC
regulation. Beyond their opposition to rulemaking itself, almost all of the industry representatives who testified voiced
their dissatisfaction with the procedural requirements of S.
986. Perhaps their most frequent complaint was that the bill
provided little guarantee against poorly reasoned decisions.
Although it did require that rules be based upon substantial
evidence in a record, there was little to ensure that this evidence would be sound without such devices as the swearing of
witnesses, discovery, cross-examination, and rebuttal.

The version of S. 986 reported out of the Senate Commerce
Committee in July of 1971 was considerably more stringent in
its procedural requirements than the original bill. Perhaps the
most significant change was the provision that a trial-like hearing would be required if written or oral comment showed a
"disparity of views concerning the material facts" upon which
the rule was based. Such a hearing would be governed by the
APA's formal requirements with the exceptions that: (1) cross-

examination could be "limited in scope and subject matter," and (2) a representative could be selected by the Commission to cross-examine for a group of participants with a common interest.[47] As S. 986 was being considered on the floor, an amendment by Roman Hruska was adopted which deleted the language empowering the Commission to limit cross-examination. With this change, the bill passed the Senate in November of 1971.

H.R. 4908, the House counterpart of S. 986, was identical in its rulemaking provisions to the Senate bill. Industry witnesses before the House Interstate and Foreign Commerce Committee said essentially the same things with regard to rulemaking and rulemaking procedure as they had before the Senate. Hearings on H.R. 4908 were more balanced than those on S. 986, however, in that there was much more input from consumer advocates. Hearings in the House were held in September of 1971—after the Senate Commerce Committee had amended the procedural requirements of S. 986, making them more judicialized. As a result, consumer witnesses spent considerable effort attacking formal rulemaking requirements. H.R. 4809 was not reported out of committee.

In the Ninety-third Congress, S. 356 was introduced by Senators Magnuson and Moss on January 12, 1973. This was nine days after the introduction of very similar legislation, H.R. 20, in the House. S. 356 included rulemaking provisions identical to those of S. 986, which had passed in the previous Congress.

The Senate Commerce Committee did not hold hearings on S. 356 but did invite written comments from interested parties. In a radical turn of events, the bill's rulemaking provisions were deleted in executive session before it was reported to the floor. The reason given for this change was a request in a letter from FTC chairman Lewis Engman to Commerce Committee chairman Magnuson. Engman felt that judicial affirmation of the Commission's rulemaking authority was imminent (an expectation that soon proved to be well founded). Given this, he argued that the Commission would be better off *without* an express delegation of rulemaking authority since it appeared from H.R. 20 and S. 356 that such a grant would be accom-

panied by procedures considerably more demanding and constraining than those of the APA's section 553. As he stated:

> In view of the pending litigation . . . the Commission would oppose
> any statutory rulemaking provision limiting the flexibility of our pres-
> ent authority. The Commission recognizes the need to achieve a bal-
> ance between procedural efficiency and procedural safeguards and
> feels that judicial affirmation of the Commission's rulemaking au-
> thority will provide the flexibility needed to develop procedures which
> strike the needed balance.[48]

Engman also argued that the hotly contested rulemaking provisions of S. 356 should be dropped in order to facilitate the
passage of needed but less controversial portions of the bill.

The Senate Commerce Committee was probably willing to
delete the rulemaking provisions of S. 356 for at least two
reasons. First, pro- and anti-regulation senators alike were
glad to be rid of such a controversial issue.[49] Second, some
members of the committee viewed the deletion of rulemaking
authority as a bargaining tool that could later be used in ne-
gotiations with the House. The Senate Commerce Committee
was, in the aggregate, more pro-consumer and pro-regulation
than its House counterpart. It is unlikely that the committee's
members ever seriously believed that the House would accede
to FTC improvement legislation which was devoid of a rulemaking provision. Rather, they probably hoped that their deletion of rulemaking could be used to help mitigate some of the
procedural requirements imposed by the House, or to gain
concessions on other aspects of the bill.[50]

The Senate had been the incubator for FTC improvement
legislation in the Ninety-first and Ninety-second Congresses.
It was there that specific proposals for FTC rulemaking procedure had been shaped through conflict and compromise. For
its part, the House Interstate and Foreign Commerce Committee had considered the issue of FTC rulemaking procedures
in its hearings, but had taken little legislative initiative. In
the Ninety-third Congress, however, the House assumed the
dominant role. To a great extent it was the House that for-

mulated the rulemaking procedures which ultimately became law as part of the Magnuson-Moss Act.

Representative John Moss, chairman of the House Interstate and Foreign Commerce Committee, introduced H.R. 20 on January 3, 1973. This legislation was similar to H.R. 4809 of the Ninety-second Congress in most respects, but its provisions for FTC rulemaking were considerably different. The procedures in H.R. 20 were the product of considerable reflection and compromise within the House Commerce Committee, and especially among the members of its Subcommittee on Commerce and Finance. Although the positions of individuals varied, there had arisen a consensus among most members that (1) the FTC needed rulemaking to protect consumers effectively, and (2) such authority should be accompanied by procedural safeguards more stringent than those of the APA's Section 553. The second of these premises was based partially on the feeling that affected parties should be afforded due process guarantees in rulemaking, since it was often there and not at the adjudicatory stage of the enforcement process that most crucial issues were decided. Relatedly, the endorsement of more rigorous procedures was also based on the realization that the unusual breadth of the FTC's mandate warranted more extensive safeguards against the possible abuse of discretion.[51]

Congressman Bob Eckhardt played the key role in shaping the rulemaking procedures of H.R. 20. Eckhardt had long been a consumer advocate. Thus, he believed that the FTC should have the authority to issue TRRs and that the efficiency of the agency's rulemaking should not be unduly constrained by procedural requirements. Yet he had also become convinced that TRRs should be promulgated under procedures more rigorous than those of the APA's Section 553.[52] In coming to this conclusion, Eckhardt may have been influenced by his perception that procedural compromise was needed if a rulemaking provision was to pass the House. More importantly, though, he sincerely believed in the virtues of due process. This was probably because he, along with other consumer advocates, had relied on the courts to achieve their goals in the past. (It is interesting in this regard that no less a consumer advocate than Ralph Nader was unable to reconcile himself to informal procedures for the same reason.)[53]

Eckhardt, as a liberal who nevertheless supported hybrid procedures, was instrumental in helping to achieve a degree of consensus in the Subcommittee on Commerce and Finance. There was considerable polarization among those subcommittee members with an active interest in FTC rulemaking. Congressman Moss was a liberal consumer advocate who favored informal procedures, while Congressmen Broyhill and Ware were pro-business conservatives who favored formal procedures (in the event that the FTC must have rulemaking authority). By acting as an intermediary, and through his own work and leadership, Eckhardt helped forge a rulemaking provision that both sides could support.[54]

As reported, H.R. 20 contained a unique package of rulemaking procedures. Some of its requirements were carryovers from previous bills, while others were new. One modification was that oral hearings *must* be held. S. 986 and H.R. 4809 (of the Ninety-second Congress) had only required oral hearings if requested. Rulemaking hearings under H.R. 20 were to be conducted informally, with the exception that an opportunity would be provided for cross-examination "to the extent and in the manner necessary and appropriate in view of the nature of the issues involved, as determined by the Commission." These limitations on cross-examination represented a compromise between the original version of S. 986 (which made no mention of cross-examination) and the version finally passed by the Senate (which required formal hearings with no limitations on cross-examination). Like previous legislation, H.R. 20 required that rules be based on substantial evidence in the record. In addition to hearing transcripts and written submissions, the bill expanded the definition of the record to include "any other information which the Commission deems relevant to the rule."

A completely new feature of H.R. 20 was the stipulation that the Commission include in its statement of a TRR's basis and purpose assessments of the extent to which proscribed acts or practices occurred and the extent to which they were unfair or deceptive. The agency was also required to estimate the costs its rule would impose on manufacturers and other affected persons. The first of these requirements was designed to ensure that the FTC did not use rulemaking to attack relatively narrow practices that should be treated through adjudication. Also, by forcing the Commission to consider the extent of deception as well as the economic effects of its rules, the drafters of H.R. 20 hoped to prevent the FTC from imposing remedies more harmful than the diseases they were designed to cure.[55]

Just as it had with the Senate, the Commission requested the House to delete rulemaking provisions from consumer legislation in the Ninety-third Congress. Engman reportedly telephoned Congressman Eckhardt for this purpose late the night before H.R. 20 was to be introduced. Understandably, Eckhardt was less than sympathetic to the Commission chairman's request, since he and others had devoted so much time and effort to developing a sound and mutually acceptable rulemaking format. Aside from sunk costs, however, it bears reemphasis that a majority of the subcommittee's members had, for one reason or another, come to feel that FTC rulemaking should be constrained by procedures more rigorous that the APA's informal requirements.[56]

After subcommittee hearings, Representative Moss introduced H.R. 7917 to the full Interstate and Foreign Commerce Committee. H.R. 7917 was a modification of H.R. 20, but with identical rulemaking provisions. In turn, the full committee reported H.R. 7917 to the House in June of 1974. The bill's procedural requirements were changed somewhat during markup. Interested parties were given an additional right to submit rebuttal evidence at hearings. An attempt was also made to define more specifically the Commission's power to limit cross-examination. Whereas H.R. 20 (and the original version of H.R. 7917) had stated that the agency must allow cross-examination "where appropriate in view of the nature of the issues involved," the marked-up version of H.R. 7917 required cross-examination "as may be required for a full and true disclosure of all disputed issues of material fact." Finally, as a catch-all provision to help expedite proceedings, the Commission was empowered to make rulings "as may be required to avoid unnecessary costs and delays" during hearings. H.R.

7917 was passed by the House by a vote of 384 to 1, with 49 abstaining on September 19, 1974. No amendments were added on the floor.

The final step in the legislative odyssey of Magnuson-Moss was the reconciliation between H.R. 7917 and S. 356, which had passed the Senate a year earlier without a rulemaking provision. As mentioned, the Senate Commerce Committee was dominated by liberal consumer advocates, whereas its House counterpart comprised a fairly representative sample of the political spectrum. Understandably therefore, modifications made at the behest of the Senate in conference were intended to mitigate the burdens imposed by the House bill's procedural requirements. Senator Frank Moss was instrumental in achieving these concessions. In pressing for more lenient requirements he was joined by his Senate colleague Warren Magnuson and by Representative John Moss. An important factor which enabled the conference committee to reach a solution was the willingness of Congressmen Eckhardt and Broyhill to compromise on the procedures they had worked so hard to shape.[57]

Several modifications were added to help the Commission limit the possible abuse or overuse of cross-examination. Whereas H.R. 7917 required cross-examination on "disputed issues of material fact," the bill reported out of conference stipulated "disputed issues of material fact which were necessary to resolve." The conference report (although not the bill itself) further attempted to define those matters appropriate for cross-examination and rebuttal as being issues of specific as opposed to legislative fact. This distinction was borrowed from the work of Kenneth Davis, who had argued that issues of legislative fact were not suited for judicial procedures.[58] The conference bill also provided that presiding officers at FTC hearings could assume responsibility for cross-examination when they deemed it appropriate. This was designed primarily to protect witnesses from hostile treatment by industry attorneys.

Aside from limitations on cross-examination, the Conference Committee added a provision to limit judicial review of rules to issues of material fact. This was intended to mitigate the requirement that agency decisions be based on the substantial evidence in the record. Since legislative facts or policy considerations were often difficult to substantiate with hard evidence, pro-regulation legislators hoped that this exemption would give the agency more policy-making freedom and flexibility. A final significant amendment to the procedures of H.R. 7917 was language indicating that the Commission could include in its rules requirements designed to prevent proscribed acts or practices. In other words, the FTC was specifically empowered to prescribe remedial actions to achieve its policy goals.

There was little floor debate on S. 356 as reported out of the Conference Committee. The bill came out on December 16, 1974 and passed the Senate and House on 18 and 19 December, respectively. The name given to S. 356 was Magnuson-Moss Warranty-Federal Trade Commission Improvement Act.[59]

The FTC's Choice of Procedures Pursuant to Magnuson-Moss

Magnuson-Moss was not the sole determinant of the rulemaking procedures used by the FTC. The statute established general requirements that the agency must fulfill, but the Commission had the discretion to choose its own specific procedures within the constraints set by the act. The format adopted by the FTC was an elaborate one, consisting of several phases.[60]

The Commission chose to issue two separate notices before hearings. The first, termed "initial notice of proposed rulemaking," would establish the terms of and the basis for the proposed rule. It would also invite interested parties to propose "disputed issues of material fact" to be designated for cross-examination and rebuttal at the hearing. A presiding officer would be assigned to conduct rulemaking proceedings at the time initial notice was published. The presiding officer, who belonged to a separate office within the Commission, would perform a number of important functions and could exercise discretionary powers to expedite decisions at several stages in the rulemaking process. Among his duties was to decide what will be designated as disputed issues of material fact.

The next step in the FTC's rules of practice was the "final notice of proposed rulemaking." Final notice would specify the time and place for an oral hearing and list the disputed issues which the presiding officer had designated. It would also inform interested parties that they must submit notification of their desire to cross-examine on specific designated issues. The purpose of this was to enable the presiding officer to group together participants with common interests for the purpose of avoiding redundancy.

After final notice came the hearing itself. The FTC's rules of practice added little beyond the terms of Magnuson-Moss with respect to this phase. The broad power which the statute gave the Commission to avoid unnecessary costs and delay was re-delegated to the presiding officer. The rules of practice also stated that parties wishing to cross-examine and rebut must show particularized need, and that they establish criteria for presiding officers to apply when deciding upon such requests.

Perhaps the most significant initiative taken by the agency in writing its rules of practice was made with respect to posthearing procedures—a topic upon which Magnuson-Moss was silent. After the hearing, the presiding officer was required to submit a report to the Commission which summarized the record and which offered his analysis of the way in which the evidence presented reflected on each of the designated issues. The FTC staff section responsible for developing the proposed rule would also prepare a report for the Commission. Their report would also analyze the record and would "make recommendations as to the form of the final rule." After the staff report there would ensue a second period during which interested parties could offer written comment. This period would last for at least sixty days.

As the rules of practice were originally promulgated, the second comment period ended rulemaking proceedings. In 1977, however, the D.C. Circuit Court proscribed *ex parte* communications between the Commission and interested parties after the conclusion of the second comment period. Industry had argued that this gave the agency staff (which was not barred from such communication) an unfair advantage. To quell this objection, the Commission added to its rules of practice a provision enabling interested parties to make oral presentations to the commissioners during the interim between the completion of the second comment period and the promulgation of a final rule.[61] There have been other changes in the FTC's rules of practice as well. In response to legislation passed in 1980, for example, it added an advance notice of proposed rulemaking before initial notice, and also incorporated provisions for publication and comment concerning preliminary and final regulatory analyses.[62]

The Commission's discretion in adopting specific rules of practice within the broader procedural constraints set by Magnuson-Moss bears emphasis. It is of interest that the agency gave notice and invited public comment before issuing these guidelines. Although the promulgation of rules of practice and procedure are exempted from the APA's Section 553 requirements, agency officials most likely felt it prudent to solicit public comment due to the controversial, politically charged nature of the issue.

The input received by the Commission concerning its rulemaking procedures under Magnuson-Moss came overwhelmingly from industry and from members of the Washington "trade bar." The gist of their comments was that the FTC should adopt procedures more judicialized than those it had proposed. For example, there was strong opposition to the provision that would allow presiding officers to limit cross-examination, and alternative language was suggested which would have restricted their power in this regard to a narrower range of issues.[63]

As finally promulgated, the FTC's rules of practice differed little from those it had proposed. However, this should not be taken as an indication that the agency was insensitive to those who desired extensive due process guarantees. The rules of practice adopted by the Commission were clearly more rigorous than they had to be given the language of Magnuson-Moss. As an illustration of this, Congress later imposed hybrid procedures on the Environmental Protection Agency almost identical to those specified by Magnuson-Moss, yet the EPA's rules of practice provided for only one notice of proposed rulemaking and did not require staff and presiding officer reports upon the completion of hearings. In addition, they placed much stricter limits upon the designation of issues for cross-examination and rebuttal.

The FTC's selection of such an elaborate format may seem

anomalous in view of its intense opposition to judicialized procedures throughout the legislative history of Magnuson-Moss. The fact that the agency exercised its discretion in this way can most likely be attributed to its uncertainty regarding Congress's intentions and to its desire to legitimate its subsequent rulemaking decisions. The legislative requirements that cross-examination and rebuttal be allowed on "issues of material fact which are necessary to resolve" and that decisions be based on the "substantial evidence contained in the rulemaking record" were far from clear, and Congress, the courts, and the public in general seemed ambivalent with regard to FTC rulemaking and rulemaking procedure.

CONCLUSION

As discussed in Chapter 1, the choice of administrative institutions is typically informed by broad normative considerations of sound government, as well as by political pressures. Certainly, both types of influence have been evident in the case of the FTC rulemaking. As one might expect, arguments for and against the agency's use of TRRs have been expressed in terms of good and legitimate administration. Thus, proponents of rulemaking have argued that it is often a fairer, more flexible, and more efficient and effective means of implementation than the case-by-case approach, while opponents have maintained that it is often insensitive to variation among regulatory contexts and that it entails the exercise of excessive bureaucratic discretion. At the same time, support for and opposition to rulemaking by consumer advocates and industry groups, respectively, reflected their anticipation that it would have important substantive policy implications as a more forceful regulatory approach than adjudication. The perceived balance of power between these two elements of the FTC's political environment has been an important determinant of the agency's willingness to issue TRRs.

Narrow group interests and genuine normative concerns have also combined to shape FTC rulemaking procedures. Consumer advocates and the Commission lobbied for informal procedures as means of expediting rulemaking, while industry groups and their legislative allies were undoubtedly motivated in large part by the expectation that formal procedures could be exploited for the purpose of delaying, discouraging, or blocking the issuance of TRRs. Yet the compromise format imposed by Magnuson-Moss also reflects sincere misgivings among even some liberal congressmen concerning the adequacy of the APA's simple notice-and-comment format as a constraint on such a broad delegation of discretionary power. Due process was attractive in this regard as a way to ensure the soundness of agency rationale and the viability of public participation. Relatedly, it was viewed as a means of strengthening the accountability of the administrative process through judicial review.

Analysis of the effects of institutional choice logically complements a consideration of its determinants. With this in mind, the next chapter examines FTC rulemaking since Magnuson-Moss. The hybrid procedures imposed by the act have significantly affected the agency's policymaking. In addition, reliance on rulemaking itself (which Magnuson-Moss encouraged) has had profound effects on the FTC's relationship with its political environment.

NOTES

1. *Federal Trade Commission v. Curtis Publishing Company*, 160 U.S. 598 (1923).

2. Rules are almost always issued in the name of consumer protection. Occasionally, however, a rule which proscribes an unfair or deceptive practice will also be justified as a means of protecting "reputable" competitors within an industry.

3. "Rulemaking Under the Magnuson-Moss Warranty-Federal Trade Commission Improvement Act," report to Congress by the Federal Trade Commission, photocopy, June, 1979.

4. A. Lee Fritschler, *Smoking and Politics* (Englewood Cliffs, New Jersey: Prentice-Hall, 1969) pp. 73–74.

5. This is perhaps best illustrated by the fact that FTC rulemaking was subsequently declared illegal by the courts on two occasions, but was eventually vindicated upon appeal. See notes 30, 31.

6. *Trade Regulation Rule for the Prevention of Unfair or Deceptive Advertising and Labeling of Cigarettes in Relation to Health Hazards*

of Smoking and Accompanying Statement of Basis and Purpose of Rule, Federal Trade Commission Document, June, 1964, p. 141.

7. *Ibid.*, see 15 U.S.C. sec. 46(g).

8. See, for example, Robert Weston, "Deceptive Advertising and the FTC," *The Federal Bar Journal* (June, 1964), pp. 566–67. Opponents of rulemaking supported the first of these points with references to the context in which Section 6(g) occurred and to the FTC Act's legislative history.

9. *Ibid.*, p. 570 (footnote).

10. Weston, *supra* note 8, pp. 568–69.

11. *Ibid.*

12. For a discussion of the advantages the FTC perceived for rulemaking see David L. Shapiro, "The Choice of Rulemaking or Adjudication in The Development of Administrative Policy," *Harvard Law Review*, 78 (1965).

13. Alan Stone, *Economic Regulation and the Public Interest: The Federal Trade Commission in Theory and Practice* (Ithaca, New York: Cornell University Press, 1977) p. 233.

14. Fritschler, *supra* note 4, p. 75.

15. *Ibid.*

16. Weston, *supra* note 8, p. 567.

17. *Report of the President's Committee on Administrative Management* (Washington, D.C.: United States Government Printing Office, 1937).

18. Stone, *supra* note 13, p. 233.

19. *Ibid.*, pp. 232–35.

20. Lucy Black Creighton, *Pretenders to the Throne* (Lexington, Massachusetts: Lexington Books, 1976) pp. 32–34.

21. Lynn Sutcliffe, "A History of the Magnuson-Moss Warranty-Federal Trade Commission Improvement Act," case study manuscript prepared for use by the Kennedy School of Public Affairs, Harvard University (1976) p. 4.

22. Representative John Moss, statement before the Subcommittee on Commerce of the House Interstate and Foreign Commerce Committee, March 30, 1973.

23. *Federal Register*, (May 1962) pp. 4611–12.

24. For an excellent discussion of the cigarette rule and the controversy surrounding it see Fritschler, *supra* note 4.

25. Weston, *supra* note 8.

26. Edward F. Cox, Robert C. Felmeth, and John E. Schultz, *The Nader Report on the Federal Trade Commission* (New York: Barron Publishing Company, 1969).

27. American Bar Association, *Report of the ABA Commission to Study the Federal Trade Commission* (ABA: 1969), p. 86.

28. See, for example, "FTC Substantive Rulemaking: An Evaluation of Past Practice and Proposed Legislation," *New York University Law Review*, 48 (1973) pp. 144–45.

29. Wayne Hagar, statement before the Consumer Subcommittee of the Senate Commerce Committee, Hearings on the Product Warranties and FTC Improvement Act of 1971, S. 986. Comm. Ser. No. 92–8.

30. *Bristol Meyers Corp. v. FTC*, 284 F. Supp. 745 (D.D.C. 1968).

31. *National Petroleum Refiners' Association v. FTC*, 482 F. 2d 672, 690 (D.C. Cir., 1973) *cert. denied*, 415 U.S. 951 (1974).

32. Barry B. Boyer, "Trade Regulation Rulemaking Procedures of the Federal Trade Commission: A Report to the Administrative Conference of the United States by the Special Project for the Study of Rulemaking Procedures Under the Magnuson-Moss Warranty-Federal Trade Commission Improvement Act," (Report presented at the Administrative Conference of the United States, Washington, D.C., 1979) ch. 2, pp. 2–3. Hereafter cited as Boyer Report.

33. See, for example, *Consumer Warranty Protection*, Hearings on H.R. 20 and H.R. 521 before the Subcommittee on Commerce and Finance of the House Interstate and Foreign Commerce Committee. Comm. Ser. No. 93–17.

34. Representative McCollister, Hearings on H.R. 20, *supra* note 33.

35. John Ware on behalf of the National Chamber of Commerce, Hearings on S. 986, *supra* note 29.

36. Mark Silbergeld, Hearings on H.R. 20, *supra* note 33.

37. Boyer Report, *supra* note 32, ch. 2, pp. 2–3.

38. Magnuson-Moss Warranty–Federal Trade Commission Improvement Act, Pub. Law No. 93–637, Tit. I, 88 Stat. 2183, 15 U.S.L. secs. 2301–12 (1976).

39. Boyer Report, *supra* note 32, ch. 2.

40. Conversation with Sutcliffe, Washington, D.C., August, 1979.

41. Boyer Report, *supra* note 32, ch. 2, pp. 2–3.

42. Winston H. Pickett on behalf of the Chamber of Commerce of the United States, Hearings on the Product Warranties and FTC Improvement Act of 1971, Before the Senate Commerce Committee, S. 986. Comm. Ser. No. 92–8. March 22, 1971.

43. Statement of Gilbert Weil. Quoted from Boyer Report, *supra* note 32, ch. 2, p. 10.

44. FTC Chairman Lewis Engman, Hearings on H.R. 20, *supra* note 33, March 19, 1973.

45. *Ibid.*

46. FTC Chairman Miles Kirkpatrick, Hearings on S. 986, *supra* note 29, March 19, 1973.

47. Boyer Report, *supra* note 32, ch. 2, p. 10.

48. Senate Report no. 83–151, 93rd Cong., 1st Sess. 6 (May 14, 1973).

49. Boyer Report, *supra* note 32, ch. 2, p. 21.

50. Conversation with Calvin Collier, August, 1979. At the time Magnuson-Moss was in Conference Committee, Mr. Collier was chief counsel for the FTC. He later became FTC chairman before retiring to private law practice.

51. Boyer report, *supra* note 32, ch. 2, pp. 24–25.

52. Conversation with Peter Kintzler, staff attorney for the House Interstate and Foreign Commerce Committee, August, 1979.

53. *Ibid.*

54. *Ibid.*

55. *Ibid.*

56. Collier, *supra* note 50.

57. *Ibid.*

58. Kenneth Culp Davis, *Administrative Law Treatise* (St. Paul, Minnesota: West Publishing Company, 1978) Sec. 6.21.

59. Named for Representative John Moss.

60. 16 C.F.R. 1.7–1.20.

61. Boyer Report, *supra* note 32, ch. 1, p. 12.

62. Federal Trade Commission Improvements Act of 1980, Pub. Law no. 96–252, 94 Stat. 374, sec. 21. These provisions will be discussed in more detail in Chapter 6.

63. For example, the Gulf Oil Company argued that the broad discretion left to presiding officers for limiting cross-examination would lead to capriciousness:

Each called hearing will be unique unto itself and the procedure governing the conduct of the hearing will depend on the individual mood and whim of whatever Presiding Officer is appointed by the Commission.... Whatever procedural rules are adopted should guarantee to every interested party the rights to a full and fair hearing.... Because there is no clear definitive standard set forth in the rules by which an objective party can determine what is appropriate, Gulf suggests that the Commission reject the proposal as written and require that such standards be set forth in any new proposal."

Letter from Gulf to FTC, May 2, 1975.

•6 The FTC's Experience Since Magnuson-Moss

Emboldened by the seemingly unambiguous mandate of Magnuson-Moss, the FTC channeled a much greater proportion of its consumer-protection resources to rulemaking. Beginning in 1975, the Commission proposed a series of ambitious new TRRs affecting a variety of important industries. Very few of these proceedings have come to fruition, however, even though most were begun in the mid–1970s. The FTC's dismal performance in rulemaking is attributable in part to an intense reaction against proposed TRRs and other policies from the business community and, somewhat ironically, from Congress. It is also due to the procedural requirements of the Magnuson-Moss Act. The Commission's experience since Magnuson-Moss illustrates the difficulties posed by an aggressive rulemaking approach within a conflictual and unstable political environment, as well as the problems inherent in using judicialized procedures to make broad legislative policy.

IMPLICATIONS OF THE COMMISSION'S EMPHASIS ON TRRs

An Aggressive Rulemaking Approach

In 1977 a representative from the FTC's Bureau of Consumer Protection responded to concerns expressed by members of the

House Judiciary Committee that the agency was not emphasizing TRRs heavily enough as a forceful consumer protection tool. She stated that the proportion of the bureau's staff resources devoted to rulemaking had risen to 21.3 percent in 1976, as compared with 10.0 percent in 1974. Beyond this, she assured the Committee that the Commission intended to rely on rulemaking even more heavily in the future.[1]

A comparison of the FTC's rulemaking activity after Magnuson-Moss with that before the act lends credence to the Bureau's statistics. Between 1962 and 1974 the Commission proposed thirty-three TRRs, twenty-six of which were finally promulgated. In contrast, the FTC proposed twenty new rules in the five years following the passage of Magnuson-Moss (and nine in 1975 alone), as well as three amendments to old TRRs. More importantly, there has been a significant qualitative escalation in the FTC's rulemaking efforts. As discussed in the preceding chapter, pre-amendment rulemaking was generally of minor significance until the late 1960s and early 1970s, when the Commission promulgated several ambitious TRRs in response to criticism from consumer advocates. Regulations proposed after Magnuson-Moss have continued this trend, extending the reach of FTC rulemaking in key respects.

One important characteristic of TRRs proposed after Magnuson-Moss is that they have often been multifaceted, consisting of several, sometimes diverse, proscriptions and/or prescriptions. In contrast, earlier rules tended to be confined to single practices or at least to more narrowly defined problems. The version of the Funeral Industry Practices Rule proposed in the agency's final staff report illustrates the substantive breadth and diversity which has characterized many of the FTC's efforts since 1975. Among other things, the rule specified that

- funeral homes provide detailed price lists concerning caskets, vaults, grave liners, and eleven other categories of goods and services. These lists would have to be made available before discussion and selection took place.

- agreements between funeral homes and consumers be made in writ-

ing and that they specify fees for at least eight categories of goods
and services.

- funeral homes not charge customers for the cost of advancing money
  to other persons providing goods or services.

- any rebates, commissions, or discounts from third parties be passed
  on from the funeral home to customers.

- funeral homes make "alternative containers" available for cremation.

- various state laws and regulations governing facilities and practices
  within the funeral industry and otherwise limiting entry and competition would no longer be valid.

As another illustration, the Ophthalmic Goods and Services
TRR (promulgated in 1978) proscribed such diverse industry
practices as bans on eye care advertising and the withholding
of prescriptions from patients.

Another important feature of Magnuson-Moss TRRs is that
they have often gone beyond traditional and widely accepted
constructions of the FTC Act. As discussed in the preceding
chapter, a handful of pre-amendment TRRs reflected a willingness to establish important new policy rather than merely to
codify old adjudicatory precedent or to attack obviously deceptive practices. Many of the TRRs proposed since 1975 have gone
further in this regard. The bases for these proceedings have
often been ambitious extensions of the "unfairness doctrine,"
a vague and open-ended concept which the Commission began
to utilize in the mid–1960s as a justification for its consumer
protection actions.[2]

In commenting on the legislative character of some rules
proposed since Magnuson-Moss, Barry Boyer asserts that some
FTC officials have inferred a broad "moral charter" from the
FTC's enabling legislation. As an illustration, he cites the proposed funeral rule, which would proscribe certain practices primarily because "they prey upon consumers at a time when they
are exceptionally vulnerable due to their grief."[3] Perhaps the
most dramatic example of the FTC's willingness to use unfairness as the basis for broad value judgments is the children's
advertising proposal (which was subsequently withdrawn). The
agency asserted that the advertising of breakfast cereals and
certain other products was inherently unfair since the sugar

in such foods had harmful health effects and since children were highly susceptible to advertising. As the rulemaking staff stated in its report, "Unfairness ... arises out of the striking imbalance of sophistication and power between well-financed adult advertisers, on the one hand, and children on the other, many of whom are too young to even appreciate what advertising is."[4] In addition to being based on a novel concept of unfairness, the children's advertising proposal attacked practices that had long been in use and that were accepted (or at least had not been questioned) by many.

The Administrative Significance of FTC Rulemaking

Rulemaking has been widely endorsed as a means of implementing policy. It is arguably fairer than case-by-case adjudication in that it permits the prospective and evenhanded application of policy to members of society. In addition, it is said to be a superior means of developing policy, since it allows decision makers to look comprehensively both at problems and at the ramifications of possible solutions. Relatedly, rulemaking is advocated as a quicker, more efficient, and more forceful way of achieving desired policy results. Although the great majority of TRRs proposed since Magnuson-Moss have yet to be issued, a consideration of the FTC's efforts both before and after the act highlights at least the potential superiority of rulemaking in most of these respects.

Efforts to achieve through adjudicatory actions policy results similar to those contemplated by many actual or proposed TRRs would often have imposed substantial inequities, arbitrarily placing those singled out for regulation at a competitive disadvantage with regard to others engaged in similar activities. The Commission does enjoy the discretion to bring adjudicatory actions against several parties at once or to delay the effectiveness of orders until actions have been brought against all those engaged in a given practice.[5] These devices are burdensome at best, however, and have been infeasible where the Commission has sought to alter widespread practices within large industries, such as it has with rules or proposed TRRs pertaining to eye care, funeral homes, games of chance, door-to-door sales, and franchising practices, among others.

Beyond considerations of fairness, TRRs have also proven to be a potentially more comprehensive and coherent way for the FTC to formulate policy. Although the Commission has in some instances attempted to go beyond the cases at hand in statements accompanying its adjudicatory decisions, the courts have often been unreceptive to such efforts.[6] In contrast, the breadth of many TRRs—and especially those issued or proposed since Magnuson-Moss—attests to the advantage of rulemaking as a device which has allowed the FTC to plan and to confront a variety or pattern of commercial practices. Certainly, the agency would have been hard-pressed to articulate in a single adjudicatory proceeding all of the policies set forth in its funeral practices proposal, for example.

By the same token, rulemaking has allowed (and in fact required) the Commission to weigh the full range of implications stemming from its proposed actions and to consider the views of all who might be affected. To be sure, many have questioned whether agency decision makers have done this competently or wisely or with sufficient rigor in many cases. Nevertheless, rulemaking proceedings have typically entailed extensive consideration of the probable social and economic effects of proposed TRRs, both by agency staff and by outside participants.

As a means of formulating comprehensive policy, rulemaking has also proven to be a more efficient and effective way for the FTC to achieve desired regulatory results. Notwithstanding some of the trivial TRRs issued in the 1960s, rulemaking has allowed the Commission to formulate broad and legally binding policy in a single stroke when it has been so inclined. Again, although policy can also be developed through adjudication, the formulation of broad, generally applicable standards in this way is usually an incremental process at best. Further, policy established via adjudication frequently suffers in terms of clarity and coherence due to the fact that is has been pieced together from individual cases.

Of course, the contention that rulemaking is a more effective or forceful means of regulation presumes not only that it is an efficient way to develop standards, but also that such standards either facilitate subsequent enforcement proceedings or that they elicit widespread voluntary compliance. To date, a TRR has never served as the basis for a formal adjudication, although the Commission has occasionally used its rules in consent order proceedings. This may be attributable to the political and legal controversy that has often surrounded the agency's rulemaking efforts or, alternatively, to the fact that TRRs have been largely self-enforcing. While there is little current evidence which reflects on this latter hypothesis, several pre-amendment TRRs were apparently successful in changing industry behavior.[7] Perhaps the strongest evidence on behalf of the potential forcefulness of TRRs as a means of regulation, however, has been the strident opposition of the business community both to particular rules and to the prospect of rulemaking in general.

Reaction against the Commission

Partly because of their breadth and their reliance on imaginative new interpretations of "unfair or deceptive," Magnuson-Moss proposals have been ambitious in another important respect: they have often stood to impose substantial burdens upon industries possessing a good deal of political influence. Among those singled out for regulation have been such large, well-organized, and well-heeled interests as the manufacturers of drugs, foods, hearing aids, textiles, plastics, and mobile homes, as well as the advertising industry and the television networks. Industries composed primarily of small but numerous and widely-dispersed firms have also been attacked. For example, every congressman's constituency has been affected by TRRs seeking to regulate used car dealers, opticians, and funeral home directors.

One should hasten to add that, aside from TRRs, other FTC actions have been politically ambitious as well. Enforcement proceedings in recent years have sometimes relied on new and controversial economic theories and have attacked members of politically influential industries. For example, about 10 percent of the Commission's efforts to police anticompetitive practices in recent years have come against doctors and other members of the health care industry. Targets of anti-trust proceedings or investigations have also included members of the insurance, cereal, dairy, and petroleum industries, among others. The reaction against the FTC and its policies has been intense. Numerous groups affected by TRRs and other actions (either real or anticipated) have pressured Congress, attacking the Commission and its policies and seeking exemptions from the agency's scrutiny. For example, the National Automobile Dealers Association gave more than $1 million in congressional campaign contributions in 1979 and 1980, largely in response to a proposed TRR that would have required used car dealers to disclose major defects and the extent of warranty coverage.[8] Similarly, a vigorous lobbying campaign was mounted against the children's advertising proposal by the breakfast food, television, and advertising industries.

FTC activism has precipitated more generally focused reactions as well. For instance, in 1979 a representative from the U.S. Chamber of Commerce expressed to Congress his concerns about the FTC's rulemaking activities in the following manner:

Perhaps more than any other Federal agency, the FTC typifies what the average American seems to be concerned about in government. Through its rulemaking powers, the FTC has involved itself in the affairs of industry and consumers stretching from one end of society to another. This omniscience raises a fundamental question: As it now exists under the FTC Act, is rulemaking prudent and consonant with the principles of government embraced by the Constitution?[9]

Michael Wines reported in 1982 that for over a year the National Association of Manufacturers and the Chamber of Commerce had been leading major lobbying groups and corporations in biweekly sessions for the purpose of devising strategies to curb the FTC.[10]

Industry's reaction against the Commission has had a substantial effect on the legislature. If Congress was pro-FTC when it passed the Magnuson-Moss Act, it was most assuredly not so by the late 1970s. As Commission chairman James Miller stated in 1982, "I just cannot tell you the depth of distrust and loathing and dislike that there is on the Hill for the Federal Trade Commission."[11] The legislature's disaffection has been accompanied by the idea that the FTC should be restrained or even emasculated. One congressman expressed this sentiment in particularly strong terms before the House Rules Committee in 1980: "Back home, the way to kill a rattlesnake is to cut its head off. That is what we ought to do today."[12] Of course, legislative policies are the final proof of Congress's mood. In this regard, the list of actual and proposed restrictions upon the Commission since the late 1970s is impressive indeed, for Congress has used practically every weapon in its arsenal to limit and punish the agency in recent years.

The most publicized effort to constrain the FTC was a legislative veto imposed by the Federal Trade Commission Improvements Act of 1980.[13] Under its provisions, the Commission was required to submit final TRRs to Congress, which would then have sixty days to review and disapprove the agency's action through a concurrent resolution (a two-house resolution not subject to the president's signature). The legislature later exercised its veto prerogative in 1982 when the Commission finally promulgated its controversial Used Car Rule.

Although the Supreme Court's *Chadha* decision in 1983 precluded continued use of Congress's veto over FTC rules in its present form, the legislature may enact some alternative mechanism which would satisfy constitutional objections on the grounds of separation of powers and presentment (to the president for his signature). One measure under consideration would require FTC rules to be approved by a joint resolution of Congress and signed by the president. Another, less extreme proposal would subject TRRs to joint resolutions of disapproval.[14]

The FTC Improvements Act of 1980 also sought to constrain or to improve the quality of the Commission's rulemaking through procedural controls that went beyond the requirements of Magnuson-Moss. One stipulation was that the FTC publish an "advance notice of proposed rulemaking" (before initial and final notice). The purpose of this was to provide earlier warning of FTC actions to interested parties (including Congress) and to ensure participation at an earlier stage in the policy making process, as the agency was considering alternative ways to achieve its regulatory objectives.

Another procedural requirement imposed in 1980 was that proposed and final TRRs be accompanied, respectively, by preliminary and final regulatory analyses. In the case of each, there had to be a "statement of the need for and the objectives of the rule," and "an analysis of the projected benefits and any adverse economic effects and other effects" of the TRR and of "other reasonable alternative approaches" as well. Furthermore, the final analysis had to include a "summary of any significant issues raised in response to the preliminary analysis" (during the comment phase of Magnuson-Moss proceedings), together with a summary of the Commission's assessment of those issues. The courts were explicitly authorized to set aside rules in cases where the FTC failed to adequately perform a regulatory analysis. These requirements were precipitated by industry lobbying and by the perception that some of the FTC's proceedings were poorly conceived. They were perhaps a predictable response by Congress given the growing popularity of cost-benefit analysis as a means of structuring regulatory discretion (see Chapter 4).

Beyond these devices, Congress has attempted to constrain FTC activities through various substantive amendments to the agency's enabling legislation. For example, in 1980 the use of unfairness as a basis for TRRs regulating advertising was suspended for a period of three years. This vague and sweeping concept had proven to be the source of many ambitious and controversial proposals, and its deletion was meant to reduce the Commission's policy-making discretion.[15] Subsequent bills have sought to eliminate the unfairness mandate permanently for all or some rulemaking, or to restrict its scope through further definition. One proposal which enjoys widespread support would limit the FTC's purview under unfairness to industry practices that cause "substantial consumer injury" that is not outweighted by their economic benefits. Beyond the elimination or modification of unfairness, other proposed amendments would restrict rulemaking to abuses that are prevalent throughout an industry and would increase the burden of economic evidence needed to issue TRRs.[16]

In addition to generally applicable substantive limitations, Congress has created exemptions from FTC regulation for a variety of groups which have protested actual or anticipated agency proceedings. In 1980, for instance, the Commission was permanently barred from regulating children's advertising on the basis of unfairness, and was prevented from issuing rules pertaining to funeral sales practices other than price disclosure, consumer deception, or illegal boycotts. Those who have benefited from full or partial exemptions from FTC rulemaking or other actions also include insurance companies, trademark holders, savings and loans associations, soft-drink bottlers, and agricultural cooperatives.[17] Other legislative proposals which have enjoyed strong support in recent years (along with strong opposition from consumer groups) would exempt doctors, lawyers, and other professional groups, as well as dairy cooperatives, from FTC scrutiny.[18]

The legislature has shown its disfavor with the FTC in yet other ways as well. One has been by placing general or particular moratoria on rulemaking and other activities. Another has been through the appropriations process. In this regard, delays and stopgap spending measures have been the norm in recent years, and the agency was even forced to shut down briefly on two occasions in 1980 due to lack of funds. Large appropriations cuts which would force the FTC to close all or some of its regional offices have also been proposed.[19]

Finally, the executive as well as Congress has reflected industry's reaction against FTC policies. As one might expect, the conservative Reagan administration has been especially sympathetic to complaints from the business community and has made strong efforts to constrain the Commission. The most important move in this regard was the appointment of James Miller as FTC chairman in September of 1981. Unlike consumer activist Michael Pertschuk, who had headed the Commission during the Carter administration, Miller is a strong believer in the free market and has long been a vocal critic of excessive regulation by the FTC and other agencies. In turn, Miller has selected a Commission staff composed of like-minded conservatives which has helped him to exercise a good deal of control over the agency's policy-making agenda. An especially important member of Miller's team is Timothy Muris, who was appointed as director of the Commission's Bureau of Consumer Protection. Also possessed of great confidence in the virtues of unrestrained competition, Muris has been highly critical of proposed TRRs and other actions as imposing economic costs more burdensome than their benefits.[20]

The Political Costs of Rulemaking

The reaction against the FTC by the business community and ultimately by Congress and the executive partly explains the Commission's dismal rulemaking performance to date. Initial notices in all twenty Magnuson-Moss proceedings appeared before 1979, and sixteen of these came out in 1975 or 1976; yet only five TRRs have been issued. Most proceedings are still in progress, although four proposed rules have been withdrawn by the Commission and one has been vetoed by Congress. Even the rules which have been finally promulgated have failed to remain intact. Two have been remanded in whole or in part by the courts, one has been partially stayed by the Commission pending a possible amendment, and one was vetoed by Congress and then reissued in substantially weaker form.[21]

The Commission's failure to promulgate final rules has obviously been due in some instances to formal intervention by Congress. As discussed, specific legislation has delayed or ended some proceedings, and in other cases has imposed restrictions which have made it necessary for the agency to reexamine and modify its proposals. Since 1981, new conservative appointees at the FTC have also been instrumental in setting aside final staff proposals (which of course must be approved by the commissioners).[22] In addition, the fact that many Magnuson-Moss rules have languished for so long has most probably been due in large part to trepidation about further alienating an already hostile environment. This assertion is, of course, difficult to substantiate with hard evidence, and indeed it was denied by former chairman Pertschuk during congressional hearings.[23] However, FTC staff as well as a variety of other informed observers have attested to the chilling effect the strong reaction against the Commission's TRRs and other policies has had on rulemaking proceedings.[24]

The difficulty encountered by the Commission in its efforts

to promulgate Trade Regulation Rules suggests that, in addition to promoting traditional administrative values, rulemaking can have important unintended consequences. Specifically, the FTC's emphasis on TRRs has had a profound effect on its relationship with its political environment. As a more forceful means of implementing the Commission's consumer-protection mandate, rulemaking has brought about an unprecedented reaction against the agency.

Of course, the importance of rulemaking in this regard should not be overstated. As mentioned, the Commission has acted aggressively through a variety of means in recent years. Ambitious adjudicatory proceedings and other actions have been initiated against members of politically powerful industries in the areas of both anti-trust and consumer protection, and these have certainly helped fuel the reaction against the Commission. Further, even to the extent that rules have been the source of the Commission's troubles, one might argue that the substance of particular TRRs rather than the agency's use of rulemaking, *per se,* has been to blame. Thus, the trivial TRRs issued in the 1960s evoked little opposition. In the same vein, some observers have argued that the FTC's difficulties under Magnuson-Moss have stemmed largely from the fact that proposed rules have been based upon overly ambitious and politically insensitive interpretations of "unfair or deceptive," or that they have otherwise been poorly reasoned and inadequately substantiated.[25]

In defense of the FTC against charges of overzealousness in rulemaking, however, one should note that decisions to emphasize TRRs—both before and after Magnuson-Moss—have come at the urging of Congress. Even some of the agency's most controversial proceedings, such as the childrens' advertising and funeral practices proposals, were initiated at the behest of legislators, although they later became a source of rebuke as allegedly going beyond statutory intent. Indeed, one of the agency's strongest critics admits that "as late as 1977 Congress was regularly chastising the Commission for moving too slowly in its rulemaking proceedings, not too aggressively."[26]

In any case, its emphasis on rulemaking has made the FTC a much more powerful consumer-protection agency, and has made efforts to police unfair or deceptive practices much more visible and salient to members of its political environment. As an industry representative stated before a House subcommittee in 1979, for example, "Rulemaking has created a lot of problems and rulemaking has recently focused a lot of attention on the Federal Trade Commission."[27] In the same authorization hearings, a member of the House supported his argument for a congressional veto over TRRs by noting that "FTC rules are in effect laws.... The FTC derives this broad and awesome rulemaking authority from one section of the Federal Trade Commission Act...."[28]

New regulation which proscribes practices already in use is bound to be controversial, especially when undertaken pursuant to a vague statutory mandate. Given this, rulemaking has clearly been significant as a way of establishing such regulation in a more precipitous manner, both in regards to its substance and its immediate applicablity. As Ernest Gellhorn and Glen Robinson note:

> the FTC's power to remedy "unfairness" in the marketplace never received as much attention when it was used to shore up adjudicatory complaints against individual advertisements as when it was used to challenge by rule a class of advertising by an entire industry. The greater immediate reach of the rule made the agency appear much more threatening....[29]

Rulemaking (or at least meaningful rulemaking) is by nature a commitment in statutory interpretation, and the FTC's history illustrates well the political difficulties inherent in making such a commitment pursuant to a vague mandate and within a conflictual environment. Although it may have been impossible for the Commission to forego rulemaking given the intense criticism it received for its passiveness in the area of consumer protection, the FTC's difficulties plausibly explain in an indirect way the oft-noted tendency for regulators to rely on adjudication before 1970.

Even to the extent that agencies develop standards within conflictual environments, it may be prudent to do so through a case-by-case approach which allows policy to be developed *in-*

crementally. Individual application decisions are less visible than rules and do not tend to create as much policy at any one point in time. Therefore, broad regulatory principles established piecemeal are likely to trigger less opposition than similar standards established in a single proceeding. Certainly the FTC has formulated much more policy through case law over the years than it has through rulemaking, yet the latter approach has brought about unprecedented opposition from regulated interests.

THE EFFECTS OF MAGNUSON-MOSS PROCEDURES

It is impossible to analyze the FTC's rulemaking performance in recent years without considering the impact of Magnuson-Moss procedures. These requirements, which were the subject of much debate, were included partly at the behest of business interests. As alleged by the Commission and by consumer advocates, at least, industry hoped that devices such as cross-examination, rebuttal, and decision making on the record would serve to delay and discourage rulemaking efforts. At the same time, due process requirements reflected the legislature's more legitimate desire to ensure that FTC rules would be well reasoned and well substantiated, and that they would take into account the input of affected interests.

Any effort to evaluate Magnuson-Moss procedures along these or any other lines is, of course, inhibited by the fact that so few final TRRs have been promulgated to date. Nevertheless, there is a good deal of preliminary evidence available concerning the effects of the act's hybrid requirements. Most notable in this regard is an extensive study supervised by Barry Boyer and conducted for Congress under the auspices of the Administrative Conference of the United States.[30] The Boyer Report and other evidence indicate that, as hoped, there has been widespread and detailed participation in FTC rulemaking proceedings. In addition, the agency has made extensive efforts to substantiate its policies, although some feel that it has not done so competently or with sufficient rigor. As feared by some, however, Magnuson-Moss procedures have also contributed to the extreme delay which has characterized FTC rulemaking. Relatedly, they have proved inappropriate for dealing with the broad policy issues presented by many proposed TRRs and have thus compounded the political difficulties inherent in rulemaking.

Reasoned and Well-Substantiated Decisions

Lon Fuller has written that "adjudication is ... a device which gives formal institutional expression to the influence of reasoned argument in human affairs. As such, it assumes a burden of rationality not borne by other forms of social ordering."[31] Certainly, the elements of adjudicatory procedure imposed by the Magnuson-Moss Act were designed in part to ensure that TRRs would be reasoned and rational. It was hoped that the factual and legal premises of proposed rules would be tested through cross-examination and rebuttal, and that the soundness of FTC decisions in these regards would be guaranteed by judicial review based upon the "substantial evidence" criterion.

Evidence concerning the effects of Magnuson-Moss procedures in ensuring reasoned and well-substantiate decisions is mixed. The Boyer Report notes at one point that in the face of considerable uncertainty and controversy concerning the way hybrid requirements should be interpreted, "the FTC took the position that trade regulation rulemaking under the Magnuson-Moss Act was still basically an investigative exercise similar to notice-and-comment rulemaking, rather than a judicialized fact-testing and theory-testing process."[32] As an alleged consequence, issues were poorly defined at the outset of rulemaking proceedings and comment was thus poorly focused. The report adds that the FTC apparently assumed that "evidentiary standards were loose and flexible, and that a relatively low level of proof was needed to support a TRR...."[33]

Timothy Muris is also highly critical of the Commission's failure to justify its proposals with more rigor. He argues that proposed TRRs have been characterized both by a lack of reliable evidence and by the absence of clear underlying theories. In the first instance, he argues that the Commission has relied heavily on anecdotes and its own expertise, and that it has often failed to collect more systematic evidence (through scientific sampling techniques and the like) concerning the prevalence and effects of industry practices and the implications of proposed solutions. In the second instance, he states that "many of [the FTC's] rulemakings were begun without (1) a clear statement of why the challenged practice violated the FTC Act (and therefore should be regulated) and (2) a clear substantive theory that specified why regulation would solve the perceived problem whereas market forces would not."[34]

Of course, an assessment of the FTC's rigor in decision making necessarily involves subjective and relativistic judgments, and there is also a good deal of evidence which suggests that the Commission has made painstaking efforts to justify its rules in some instances. The Ophthalmic proceeding (one of three to be completed under Magnuson-Moss) illustrates the care the Commission has taken to substantiate some of its policies. Essentially, the proposed rule consisted of two parts. One was a restriction on the advertising of goods (eyeglasses, contact lenses, etc.) and services (examinations, fittings, etc.) by ophthalmologists, optometrists, and opticians. The other was a requirement that ophthalmologists and optometrists give copies of prescriptions to their patients. A common practice among examiners had been to withhold prescriptions as a means of ensuring that patients would come to them for eyewear and fitting. It was hoped that these proposed measures would enable consumers to shop comparatively and that they would enhance competition (and thus lower consumer prices) within the eye care industry.

In order to evaluate the efficacy of the rule's proposals for achieving its stated objectives, the presiding officer's designation of issues included the following questions to resolve:

- How prevalent were advertising restrictions within the eye care industry, and how had they affected consumer knowledge?
- How had such restrictions affected competition within the eye care industry?
- What would be the effect of removal of price restrictions on competition?

- Would the removal of advertising restrictions reduce the quality of goods and services in the eye care industry?

- What would be the economic effect on small businesses and consumers of removing advertising restrictions?

- What would be the effect of requiring that examiners provide prescriptions on competition, the consumer's ability to comparison shop, and the quality of goods and services?[35]

The premises concerning the likelihood that the proposed eye care rule would achieve its stated objectives, as well as the rule's possible costs to society, were subsumed within this set of questions.

The rulemaking staff's final report to the commissioners addressed most of these designated issues through empirical evidence in the record. For instance, it cited economic studies comparing prices of eyewear in states which allowed advertising with prices in states where advertising was forbidden, and it marshalled evidence from several surveys which measured the knowledge of various categories of consumers concerning the availability of opthalmic goods and services. Technical issues were also treated in a rigorous fashion. Studies were cited which measured the effects of faulty or misprescribed lenses in response to the contention that requiring examiners to give prescriptions to their patients would prove harmful.

All of this is not to say that the ophthalmic rule was based exclusively on empirical evidence. Some issues did not readily lend themselves to rigorous testing, as, for example, the question of whether or not advertising would lead to a loss of professionalism within the eye care industry. In such cases an extensive effort was made to obtain a wide sampling of expert opinion.

Various rough measures of the Commission's efforts under Magnuson-Moss requirements also seem to suggest that the agency's decision making has been characterized by considerable research and reflection. For instance, pre-hearing investigations have typically taken a year or two to complete and have often resulted in lengthy staff reports justifying proposed rules. Likewise, final staff reports, written after the completion of hearings, have taken an average of about twenty months to complete and have often been several hundred pages in length. The FTC reported that it expended an average of 22,062 man-hours in each of its first fifteen proceedings *after* initial notice of proposed rulemaking.[36]

Whether such efforts have been induced by judicialized requirements is difficult to ascertain. Similar data on pre-amendment rulemaking are not available, and even if they were, comparisons would be risky due to the increased ambitiousness of Magnuson-Moss proposals. (One would hope that the agency did not devote 22,062 man-hours to the formulation of its sleeping bag or extension ladder rule.) Bearing this caveat in mind, however, data on the size of rulemaking records before and after Magnuson-Moss have been collected by the Boyer staff, and the contrast is striking (see Table 6.1). Whereas the agency's pre-amendment records averaged 3,123 pages in length, the first fourteen records compiled under hybrid procedures have averaged 71,174 pages. It is also instructive that FTC staff submissions have comprised 62 percent of these latter documents, as opposed to 34 percent of the records compiled before Magnuson-Moss. Perhaps more noteworthy is the fact that even the records of those pre-amendment rules considered to be very ambitious were quite short by Magnuson-Moss standards. Thus, the records for the cigarette advertising, door-to-door sales, and consumer claims TRRs were 4,696, 2,154, and 5,812 pages, respectively. Only three pre-amendment records exceeded 6,000 pages.[37]

Of course, evidence that the FTC has expended a good deal of effort in its rulemaking proceedings does not demonstrate the soundness of its decisions. Again, the Commission's critics have claimed that records have been unfocused, that the quality of the evidence and reasoning has been poor, and generally that the agency has expended its efforts attempting to justify bad policies already decided upon. Notwithstanding any alleged failings in justifying *proposed* rules, however, it is judicial review that serves as the ultimate guarantor of reasoned decision making under Magnuson-Moss. A key point in this regard is that even if the Commission has taken a lax approach concerning the standard of proof needed to support its rules, the courts have not.

Table 6.1
Size of Rulemaking Records
(in pages)

	Average Length	Median Length	% Staff Submissions
Pre–Magnuson-Moss Rulemaking	3,123	2,077	34
Magnuson–Moss Rulemaking	64,850*	51,829*	62

*These figures represent the records accumulated in the first sixteen Magnuson–Moss proceedings.

As mentioned, two of the five TRRs promulgated pursuant to Magnuson-Moss have been wholly or partially remanded (although in the case of one—the Opthalmic TRR—the decision was based primarily on a subsequent Supreme Court ruling which eroded the basis for the FTC's action).[38] In both opinions reviewing courts have made strong reference to the need for rigor in FTC rulemaking given the heightened demands for factual substantiation expressed in the Magnuson-Moss Act and accompanying congressional hearings and reports. For example, in overturning a section of the vocational schools TRR which required that a pro rata refund be given to students who drop out of courses, the Second Circuit Court stated that

when Congress, after being informed that the Commission was "strongly opposed" to the substantial evidence standard of review, nonetheless incorporated that standard in the statute,... it obviously intended that a Commission rule not receive judicial approval "unless the Commission's action was supported by the substantial evidence in the record taken as a whole...."
This Court is obligated to take a close look at what the Commission has done and to determine whether it has articulated a "rational connection between the facts found and the choice made...." We have taken a close look, and we find no rational connection between the Commission's universally applicable refund requirements and the prevention of specifically described unfair deceptive enrollment practices.[39]

Public Participation

If Magnuson-Moss procedures were designed to promote well-reasoned decisions, they were also intended to further public participation in FTC rulemaking. Indeed, Congress assumed that the latter goal would support the former, since participation would be focused upon the premises for proposed regulations. The APA's notice-and-comment requirements had, at a minimum, provided interested parties an opportunity to submit written comment, and in practice the agency had almost always conducted hearings. But one of the main virtues claimed for judicialized procedures was that they would guarantee the viability of public participation. Cross-examination and rebuttal would afford meaningful opportunities to challenge agency premises, and judicial review based on the record would ensure that the FTC took relevant arguments into account. Further, the intervener funding program was designed to aid those who lacked the resources to present their views effectively. Apparently mindful of Congress's desire that TRRs reflect widespread participation, the FTC promulgated elaborate rules of practice pursuant to Magnuson-Moss which allowed for public input throughout its decision-making process (see Chapter 5).

Have Magnuson-Moss requirements promoted the kind of participation and responsiveness Congress hoped they would? Certainly the Commission has provided substantial opportunities for written and oral comment by affected interests. Data collected in 1979 show that the FTC allowed an average of 394.6 days for prehearing written comment and 30.5 days for hearing testimony in its first sixteen Magnuson-Moss proceedings. The agency also allowed an average of 82.1 days for posthearing comment in the ten proceedings that had progressed through that stage. Given these opportunities, moreover, participation has been extensive. The number of pre- and posthearing comments received by the FTC averaged 1804.1 and 397.3, respectively, and the average number of hearing witnesses was 137.1. Furthermore, participation has been well balanced among different types of interests. In seven rulemaking hearings examined in the Boyer Report, for example, 10.6 percent of the participants were individual consumers, 7.1 percent were representatives of consumer organizations, 24.1 percent were retailers or fee professionals, 4.3 percent were manufacturers or wholesale suppliers, 7.7 percent were representatives of trade or professional associations, 4.8 percent were representatives of occupational licensing boards, and 10.9 percent were representatives of other governmental entities.[40]

Measures of participation in rulemaking proceedings do not, of course, tell us whether interested parties have been effective in influencing FTC decisions. Agency responsiveness is a separate question, and one which is much more difficult to examine objectively. In attempting to address this and other issues, Boyer and his colleagues administered a survey questionnaire to the participants in four Magnuson-Moss proceedings. The study found that "the witnesses expressed generally positive attitudes about the hearing procedures." Four out of five perceived that the opportunity for oral participation provided a significant advantage (over written comment) for those who wished to influence agency decisions, and a substantial majority also favored cross-examination.[41]

Yet at the same time, a sizeable minority of the respondents had strong reservations about the FTC's objectivity and open-mindedness. Thus, the Boyer Report notes that:

> more than a third agreed with the proposition that the outcome had already been decided before the hearing began. In addition, approximately half felt that the FTC staff had taken an adversary position during their testimony, and almost twenty percent felt that the Presiding Officer had shown favoritism toward some witnesses or points of view.[42]

As one might expect, negative perceptions were prevalent among representatives of industries and professions opposed to the proposed TRRs rather than among consumer advocates—an observation which illustrates the inherent limitations imposed by the subjectivity of the survey approach in this instance.

As with the issue of reasoned decision making, however, analysis of rulemaking proceedings still in progress is insufficient as a final basis for assessing responsiveness under Magnuson-Moss requirements. Written comment, oral testimony, cross-examination, and rebuttal are all contained in the record, and again it appears as if the courts intend to impose a high level of accountability on the Commission in justifying its TRRs in the face of competing evidence. When the Second Circuit overturned a disclosure requirement contained in the vocational schools rule, for instance, it relied on evidence introduced by an industry member which suggested that schools would be forced to underrepresent the success of their graduates to prospective students. As it stated:

Proof in the record shows that adherence to the Commission's Rule would require one school to show a job placement rate of 5.8 percent, when in fact the true employment success rate of those who responded to the school's inquiry was 54 percent, or 80 percent, if those who became self-employed were included. Another school would have to show a placement figure of approximately 67 percent, although almost 100 percent of its graduates who sought employment obtained it.[43]

Delay

If Magnuson-Moss procedures have helped to ensure that FTC decision making is reasoned and that it is sensitive to public input, they have also had undesirable side effects. The most obvious of these has been delay (see Table 6.2). Again, sixteen TRRs were proposed in 1975 and 1976, and the remaining four Magnuson-Moss proceedings were begun in 1977 and 1978, but only six rules have been finally promulgated. In contrast, the average time between initial notice and final promulgation for the twenty-four pre–Magnuson-Moss rules was 20.3 months. Moreover, this latter figure is somewhat misleading, since the Commission's rulemaking activities almost came to a standstill during litigation over the octane rule and the subsequent anticipation that Congress would change FTC procedures. Excluding the seven proceedings that were probably affected in these ways, the average time per pre–Magnuson-Moss rule drops to 14.1 months. Further excluding the anomalous light bulbs proceeding, which lasted over six years, the remaining pre-amendment rules took an average of 10.4 months to promulgate.[44]

Table 6.2

Time Required to Promulgate Pre–Magnuson-Moss Rules
(From Notice of Proposed Rulemaking)

| | Number of Months | | | | |
	1–6	7–12	13–18	19–24	25 & over
Number of Rules	4	9	3	1	7

Average time rule: 20.3 months
Median time rule: 14.2 months

Source: Data Appendix to the Boyer Report.

Note: Four of the proceedings in this category took place during a period in
which they can be presumed to have been affected by either the octane
case or Congress's pending imposition of new procedures on the FTC.
These four rules took 33.3, 39.8, 57.8, and 48.8 months to promulgate.

It bears emphasis that delay in rulemaking has not been due
solely to hybrid procedures. As discussed, some of the Commission's proposed TRRs have inspired strong criticism as well
as intense lobbying efforts by industry. In response, Congress
has intervened to block or limit a few of the FTC's efforts, and
informal pressure coupled with the FTC's desire to avoid further rebuke have undoubtedly caused the agency to proceed
more slowly and cautiously in general. One should also note
that TRRs proposed since Magnuson-Moss have, on the whole,
been more complex, with much more extensive and diverse
probable effects than pre-amendment rules. Other things being
equal, more ambitious policies should obviously entail longer
consideration.

It is impossible to assign relative importance to the various
factors that have led to such protracted rulemaking proceedings. Indeed, their effects have likely been interrelated, as will
be discussed shortly. Nevertheless, the requirement imposed
by Magnuson-Moss that TRRs be substantiated with evidence
which has been tested through the adversary process has undoubtedly been a significant source of delay. This is evidenced
by the extensive and time-consuming efforts the FTC has made
to justify its rules described earlier. Another point that bears

reiteration is that even pre-amendment TRRs considered to be very ambitious failed to generate efforts at substantiation remotely comparable to those which have accompanied their Magnuson-Moss brethren. As the Boyer Report states in regard to delay under hybrid procedures (apparently contradicting its earlier claim that the FTC has taken a lax approach under Magnuson-Moss):

There seems to be a substantial and perhaps irreducible cost in moving from the relatively discretionary decision-making of the pre-amendment TRR proceedings to the reasoned, explained, and record-supported regulatory decisions characteristic of hybrid rulemaking. Gathering large quantities of data, analyzing them and explaining the conclusions arrived at are labor-intensive processes....[45]

Delay has occurred throughout FTC rulemaking. The Commission's multistage process for alerting the public, identifying designated issues, and collecting written and oral comment has certainly been protracted in comparison with informal proceedings. Thus, the average time span between initial notice of proposed rulemaking and the completion of hearings has been almost seventeen months.[46] The expectation of due process embodied in the Magnuson-Moss Act explains the elaborate nature of the Commission's procedures for framing issues and collecting decisional input. Fear of reversal on procedural grounds also likely explains the fact that presiding officers have tended to be liberal in approving motions by participants to extend various phases of rulemaking.

It is difficult to prove, of course, that industry has exploited due process requirements with the intention of delaying Magnuson-Moss proceedings before and during rulemaking hearings. Certainly, many feel that this has been the case, arguing that lawyers have sometimes been able to save their clients millions of dollars by stalling the promulgation of TRRs which attack profitable industry practices. To quote the Boyer report: "Tactically some rule-opponents may well have argued for adjudicatory rights for the purpose of delaying the proceedings or building reversible error for judicial review. The novelty and complexity of the statutory procedures created a fertile field for opponents to use these tactics for defeating or postponing regulation."[47] Or, as one high-ranking FTC official noted, "lawyers love Magnuson-Moss procedures. Each additional day in hearings is a dollar saved for their clients and a dollar earned for themselves."[48] As a practical observation, presiding officers have often been inundated with motions of various sorts. It is perhaps also worth noting in this regard that the Practicing Law Institute has published a book which is a virtually undisguised discussion of delaying strategies available to corporate practioners under Magnuson-Moss.[49] As an aside, however, cross-examination, *per se*, has not proved to be the bête noire that the FTC and its supporters had feared. While hearings themselves have lasted almost four months on the average, close observers feel that cross-examination has increased the length of proceedings by only about two weeks in most cases.[50]

By far the greatest delay under Magnuson-Moss has come during the deliberative stages of the rulemaking process. This is obvious, since hearings have been completed in the great majority of the Commission's proceedings for several years. After the close of hearings, the presiding officer and responsible staff section must prepare separate reports based on the record. Normally, the presiding officer's report has been issued first, and its findings on disputed issues have served as a partial basis for the staff's recommended course of action. The time spent preparing these documents has been considerable: for those completed, an average of almost two years from the end of hearings to the submission of the staff's recommendation. Following the final staff report there is a period for post-record comments (those completed have lasted less than three months on the average), then a period during which the director of the Bureau of Consumer Protection formulates his own recommendation for the Commission. Finally, oral presentations are made before the Commission prior to its final decision. Most rulemaking proceedings still in progress are stalled at one of these latter stages.

A significant portion of delay in the posthearing stages of FTC rulemaking has been due to the apprehension that proposals have not been adequately justified on the basis of evidence in the record. This fear has been made more palpable by the D.C. Circuit's exacting interpretation of the Magnuson-Moss Act's substantial evidence criterion, as well as by Congress's reaction against some of the agency's initiatives. Thus, in explaining the FTC's failure to promulgate final rules, Michael Pertschuk noted in 1980 that the Commission had increased its demands on staff for analysis and supporting evidence.[51] It is especially in this context that Magnuson-Moss procedures have proved to be an invaluable strategic resource for opponents of regulation. They have strengthened the hand of industry groups as potential challengers of agency actions before the courts and have thus made it more incumbent upon the Commission to develop tight cases.

Again, one should emphasize that there are probably several explanations for the Commission's failure to promulgate rules in a more expeditious manner. Political pressures have been an important deterrent in some cases and, in addition, commissioners and other high-ranking agency officials have simply developed reservations about the wisdom of some staff proposals. This latter explanation has become especially important as the ideological orientation of the FTC has changed during the Reagan administration. Further, delay may be due in part to the Commission's imprudence in implementing Magnuson-Moss requirements rather than to the act's procedures themselves. Both Muris and Boyer argue that the FTC's failure to articulate clear legal theories and more precisely defined designated issues at the outset of rulemaking proceedings has led to poorly organized and poorly focused records and that this, in turn, has added significantly to the agency's analytical burden.

Allegations that the agency's difficulties stem from its failure to articulate clear legal and factual premises for TRRs at the beginning of proceedings actually underscore the delaying effects of Magnuson-Moss procedures in an important sense, however. Many of the rules proposed under the act have been based upon complex and value-laden policy judgments, and have therefore not lent themselves to the sort of rigorous, *a priori* justification demanded by judicialized procedures. In this regard, perhaps the most significant effect of Magnuson-Moss requirements is that they have limited the Commission's ability to exercise legislative discretion.

The Restriction of Legislative Discretion

Congress anticipated that judicialized procedures might prove inflexible for dealing with some of the issues the FTC would confront in rulemaking. At the time, in fact, there had already been a good deal of criticism of formal rulemaking procedures used by other agencies. In an attempt to prevent this problem, the Magnuson-Moss Act stipulated that due process constraints would only pertain to "issues of material fact which are necessary to resolve." By implication, at least, Congress felt that the Commission should be free to deal with broad policy issues in a more informal manner. The Conference Committee report attempted to clarify the act's intent in this regard by distinguishing between issues of specific and legislative fact (see Chapter 5).

Despite Congress's desire to facilitate policy judgments, its "material fact" proviso has had little effect in reducing the FTC's decisional burden. Boyer attributes this to the agency's failure to articulate clear legal theories for its rules. He argues that without such guidance, presiding officers have found it "impossible to determine with any precision whether the issues proposed by the parties were material or necessary to resolve."[52] However, the failure of presiding officers to limit the applicability of due process constraints has also been due to the fact that relevant issues have often not been discrete, but rather have been inextricably tied together. Commenting on the difficulty of distinguishing issues of material fact from other considerations in the context of actual proceedings, the presiding officer for the childrens' advertising rule wrote that

a bright line separation between so-called "adjudicative" and "legislative" facts cannot be accomplished in a manner consistent with Magnuson-Moss, or at least it would be hazardous to place a blanket reliance on the distinction (even if, theoretically, it could be accomplished) as determining when cross-examination is appropriate under the statute.[53]

As a result of these difficulties, presiding officers have been reluctant to exclude any relevant premises for TRRs from the category of designated issues for fear of reversal by the courts on procedural grounds.[54]

Given that rulemaking decisions have fallen almost entirely within the constraints of judicialized procedures, the effect has been to preclude or at least to discourage certain types of considerations as legitimate bases for TRRs. In this regard, the primary virtue of due process—that it has promoted well-reasoned and well-substantiated decisions—has perhaps served as its primary defect as well.

The requirement that rules be based on evidence in the record which has been tested through the adversary process is based on the assumption that legislative goals are clearly discernable and that agency actions should therefore be evaluated objectively in terms of set criteria. By thus institutionalizing an instrumental model of decision making, Magnuson-Moss procedures have made agency expertise, as such, irrelevant as a basis for TRRs (at least within the context of judicial review based on substantial evidence). This, in turn, has severely limited the Commission's ability to rely on its own informed judgment in dealing with "polycentric" policy problems, the complexity of which precludes tight, empirically justifiable solutions.[55]

Even more importantly, perhaps, due process requirements have rendered irrelevant the values or preferences of affected interests. As the Boyer Report states: "The statute's emphasis on reasoned decision making and opportunities to challenge the factual basis for the rule seems to focus the attention of the agency almost exclusively on the question of whether a proposed rule is logically and factually supportable rather than on its acceptability to affected interests."[56] In a related vein, Magnuson-Moss procedures have also discouraged the use of legislative modes of conflict resolution. The adversary process is designed to judge legal theories and actions taken pursuant to them as being either right or wrong—to select one adversary's position over the other's. By its nature, therefore, it provides neither the incentive nor the latitude for participants or decision makers to seek compromise solutions. In these respects, judicialized procedures have made it difficult for the FTC to fashion politically acceptable policies.

One specific way in which Magnuson-Moss procedures have contributed to political inflexibility is that they have encouraged participants (including agency staff) to assume a combative rather than a conciliatory posture on proposed rules. Thus, the polarizing effect of due process requirements has not only militated against compromise but has also raised the level of hostility against the Commission.[57] In addition, the prospect of altering TRRs has necessarily threatened the integrity of judicialized proceedings by introducing new premises which are not directly supported by evidence in the record and which have not been subject to testing through the adversary process. This is not to say that Magnuson-Moss procedures have precluded the modification of proposed rules. They have, however, served to delay change, again contributing to the acrimony which has surrounded FTC rulemaking. Relatedly, they have limited the options available to the Commission. Because of the costs associated with justifying new proposals and affording new opportunities for outside parties to challenge them, the Commission has often resorted to the crude device of dropping whole sections from rules as a vehicle for compromise.

As a final impediment to political expediency, Magnuson-Moss requirements have been interpreted in such a way as to place severe restrictions on *ex parte* contacts. The D.C. Circuit Court's insistence on procedural guarantees of neutrality in its 1977 *Home Box Office* decision was an important influence in this regard,[58] as was a 1978 district court ruling which disqualified Chairman Pertschuk from the childrens' advertising proceeding because of his public statements in support of the rule. Although the Commission's total ban on *ex parte* contacts (issued in 1977) has been softened somewhat, all communications outside of formal rulemaking proceedings must still be placed in the record. The significance of this is that it has further limited the agency's flexibility in achieving compromise and consensus among competing interests by placing all considerations within the rigid context of judicialized proceedings.

A common view among students of the administrative process is that because of the constraints they impose, adjudicatory procedures are only appropriate in areas where decision making is guided by clear objective standards and where it involves relatively narrow issues which lend themselves to empirical testing. Where these conditions do not obtain, judicialized procedures tend to preclude the sorts of considerations and processes which should naturally provide the basis for decisions. The FTC's experience supports this view. While Magnuson-Moss procedures have added rigor to the consideration of factual issues in rulemaking, they have been inappropriate for dealing with the political or value judgments which have undergirded many of the Commission's TRRs.

Indeed, the tension between the decisional premises and processes relevant to proposed TRRs on the one hand and the imperatives of judicialized procedures on the other helps explain the delay which has characterized FTC rulemaking. Magnuson-Moss procedures have made it incumbent to provide rational justifications for TRRs when, in fact, some rule premises have not been amenable to logical and empirical substantiation. Thus, the Commission has been reluctant to finalize some rules for fear of reversal by the courts. Similarly, the fact that due process requirements have impeded the Commission's ability to fashion politically acceptable compromises has also undoubtedly been a source of delay.

Whether the constraints on legislative discretion imposed by Magnuson-Moss procedures are good or bad depends in part on one's perspective. If the FTC should not behave like a legislature, then due process requirements may be desirable as a means of keeping the agency within traditional administrative (as opposed to political) parameters. On the one hand, they permit rules involving clear-cut and non-controversial interpretations of "unfair or deceptive" and verifiable factual assertions to be promulgated in a relatively expeditious manner. This was the case with the Commission's r-value proceeding (involving the advertising of home insulation products), for example, which was based on narrow, technical premises. On the other hand, judicialized procedures serve to delay and discourage proposed TRRs which involve broad policy issues.

As a practical matter, of course, many rulemaking proposals have presented complex factual issues which have not readily lent themselves to verification, as well as controversial value judgments which have not been obvious extensions of the FTC Act. In this regard, criticisms of the Commission for its failure to provide the rigorous supporting evidence and clear legal theories demanded by Magnuson-Moss can, in considerable measure, be rephrased as criticisms of the agency's proposals themselves, and as allegations of their inappropriateness within the context of judicialized proceedings. In defense of the FTC, one should again bear in mind that the agency's aggressive posture in general and some of its most politically ambitious policies in particular were initially encouraged by Congress. If some of the FTC's rules have proved to be too controversial, therefore, it is at least debatable whether the agency always could or should have been more careful in avoiding the political repercussions of its proposals.

In any case, the Commission's mandate is so vague and open-ended that significant policy initiatives developed through the precipitous mechanism of rulemaking are almost inevitably bound to involve controversial value judgments. As even a harsh critic of the FTC observed, what is unfair or deceptive is largely "in the eye of the beholder."[59] Thus one can argue that Magnuson-Moss procedures, which were intended to promote efficient policies in a technical sense, have been inefficient from a policy-making standpoint given the legislative character of FTC rulemaking.

CONCLUSION

Rulemaking was adopted by the FTC in the early 1960s and was emphasized in the 1970s as an effective way to police unfairness and deception and thus meet increased demands for consumer-protection policy. Unlike adjudication, which was perceived to be limited by its essentially reactive and incremental nature, rulemaking was viewed as a device which would allow the FTC to develop broad standards (in terms of both their applicability and their substance) in a single stroke. TRRs were further justified on the grounds of fairness, since they would arguably preclude retroactivity and inequity in the application of policy.

The FTC's experience confirms at least the potential superiority of rulemaking as an effective means of implementation. Precisely because of the effectiveness of rulemaking, however, its emphasis by the Commission has precipitated unprecedented opposition from regulated industry. A handful of ambitious TRRs promulgated in the late 1960s and early 1970s demonstrated to industry the forcefulness of rulemaking as a regulatory tool. As a result, the political significance of TRRs became evident during hearings on the Magnuson-Moss Act and the bills which preceded it. More recently, the spate of rules proposed since the passage of Magnuson-Moss has triggered an intense reaction against the Commission. One might argue that the FTC's problems are attributable to the insensitivity of its proposals, yet the use of rulemaking itself, pursuant to such a vague mandate, has clearly been a source of political conflict.

Its emphasis on rulemaking has necessarily forced the Commission to deal with complex and controversial issues. Congress realized that this would be the case as it was considering an explicit grant of rulemaking authority in Magnuson-Moss, and partly because of this, it imposed due process constraints on the FTC as a guarantee that rulemaking discretion would be exercised in an acceptable manner. Requirements that the agency provide opportunities for cross-examination and rebuttal and that it base its final decisions on the substantial evidence in the record were designed to ensure, ultimately through judicial review, that rules were well substantiated. Judicialized procedures were also intended to ensure that interested parties had viable opportunities to participate in FTC proceedings.

Due process requirements have, in fact, added to the formal objectivity of FTC rulemaking and have likely added to the effectiveness of public participation in some respects. At the same time, however, they have contributed to the extreme delay (and in many cases deadlock) which has characterized FTC rulemaking. Relatedly, they have also impeded the Commission's ability to deal effectively with the controversial political issues inherent in most of its proposed TRRs. As procedures designed to ensure narrow technical accountability, Magnuson-Moss requirements have focused the attention of the FTC and the courts on the factual and legal predicates of its rules to the exclusion of affected values, as such. By the same token, the inflexibility of the adjudicatory model has severely inhibited the Commission's ability to achieve accommodation among competing interests, thus exacerbating the political costs inherent in rulemaking itself.

The FTC's experience since Magnuson-Moss obviously presents a certain paradox. The emphasis on rulemaking—encouraged by Congress as a more powerful means of regulation—has added greatly to the political or legislative character of the agency's activities, while due process requirements have inhibited those sorts of considerations appropriate for legislative decision making. Jeremy Rabkin notes this irony and suggests that if Magnuson-Moss procedures were intended to legitimate the exercise of broad policy-making discretion by the FTC, they may ultimately have the opposite effect by creating unrealistic expectations of rationality in the administrative process. As he states, "The effort to invest administrative rulemaking with the aura of impartial expertise is far more likely to promote public cynicism about regulatory agencies than public respect about their decisions."[60] Moreover, the inherent inefficiency of judicialized procedures for dealing with political issues may also serve to undermine public confidence in the administrative process by limiting the ability of agencies to promulgate sound and timely regulations.

NOTES

1. Margery Smith, statement before the Commerce, Consumer, and Monetary Affairs Subcommittee of the House Government Operations Committee. Oversight Hearings Into the Federal Trade Commission—Bureau of Consumer Protection (Delays in Rulemaking-Regulation of Advertising). March 9, 1977.

2. See, for example, Dorsey D. Ellis, Jr., "Legislative Powers: FTC Rule Making," in Kenneth W. Clarkson and Timothy J. Muris, eds., *The Federal Trade Commission Since 1970: Economic Regulation and Bureaucratic Behavior* (Cambridge: Cambridge University Press, 1981) pp. 163–80.

3. Barry B. Boyer, "Too Many Lawyers, Not Enough Practical People," *Law and Policy Quarterly* 5 (January, 1983) p. 19.

4. Quoted from Senate Report No. 96–500. The Federal Trade
Commission Act of 1979. Report Together with Additional Views.
Subcommittee on the Consumer of the Senate Committee on Com-
merce, Science and Transportation. 96th Cong., 1st Sess. p. 2.

5. David L. Shapiro "The Choice of Rulemaking or Adjudication
in the Development of Administrative Policy," *Harvard Law Review*,
78 (1965) pp. 938–39.

6. *Ibid.*

7. In 1967 the Commission reported the results of two surveys of
industry members, one on compliance with a rule on the advertising
of television screen sizes, and the other on compliance with a TRR
prohibiting the use of the word "automatic" to describe sewing ma-
chines. Both surveys found total compliance (as perhaps one might
expect). "FTC Substantive Rulemaking: An Evaluation of Past Practice and Proposed Legislation," note, *NYU Law Reivew*, 48 (1973) p.
159. In addition, several informed observers have noted the powerful
effects of some pre-amendment rules in changing industry behavior.
For example, former commissioner Philip Elman cited the television
screen rule and a TRR prohibiting use of the word "leakproof" to
describe dry cell batteries as having been very effective in achieving
their desired effects. Philip Elman, "Administrative Reform in the
Federal Trade Commission," *The Georgetown Law Journal*, 59 (1971)
p. 829.

8. Michael Wines, "FTC About-Face under Miller May Not Be
Enough for Congressional Critics," *National Journal* (June 5, 1982)
p. 992.

9. Statement of Jeffrey H. Joseph, Director, Government and Regulatory Affairs, Chamber of Commerce of the United States. Author-
izations for the Federal Trade Commission and General Oversight
Issues. Hearings Before the Subcommittee on Consumer Protection
and Finance of the Committeee on Interstate and Foreign Commerce
of the U. S. House of Representatives. 96th Cong. 1st Sess. Ser. No.
96–35, p. 69.

10. Michael Wines, "Doctors, Dairymen Join in Effort to Clip the
Talons of the FTC," *National Journal* (September 18, 1982) p. 1589.

11. Quoted from Wines, *supra* note 8, p. 993.

12. Representative James H. Quillen (R-Tenn.) Before the House
Rules Committee. Hearings Concerning the Transfer of Temporary
Funds to FTC Employees. March 25, 1980. Quoted from *Congres-
sional Quarterly Weekly Report*, (March 29, 1980), p. 873.

13. Federal Trade Commission Improvements Act of 1980, Pub. L.
No. 96–252, sec. 21, 94 Stat. 374.

14. For a discussion see Michael Wines, "Legislative Veto Debate Threatens to Hogtie FTC Reauthorization Bill," *National Journal* (September 10, 1983) pp. 1830–31.

15. Federal Trade Commission Improvements Act of 1980, *supra* note 13. Also see Senate Report, *supra* note 4.

16. For a discussion of these proposals and others see, for example, Wines, *supra* notes 14 and 10.

17. Federal Trade Commission Improvements Act of 1980 *supra* note 13.

18. Wines, *supra* note 10.

19. *Ibid.*, p. 1593.

20. See, for example, Clarkson and Muris, *supra* note 2. Also, Muris, "Rules without Reason: The Case of the FTC," *Regulation Magazine* (September/October, 1982).

21. The Commission's vocational schools TRR was remanded in *Katherine Gibbs School (Inc.) v. FTC*, 612 F.2d 658 (1979), and a portion of the Ophthalmic Rule was remanded in *American Optometric Association v. FTC*, 626 F.2d 896 (1980). In addition, portions of the home insulation TRR have been stayed pending the FTC's considerations of some possible amendments. The used car rule was disapproved by Congress in 1982, but a weaker version was promulgated in December of 1984 after the Supreme Court had declared the legislative veto unconstitutional.

22. Wines, *supra* note 8.

23. *Washington Post* (May 28, 1980) p. D7, col. 4. Taken from Barry B. Boyer et al., *Phase II Report on the Trade Regulation Rulemaking Procedures of the Federal Trade Commission.* (Report prepared for Congress by the Administrative Conference of the United States. June, 1980). p. 52, footnote 158. Hereafter cited as Boyer Report, Phase II.

24. Author's conversation with FTC staff, August, 1979. Also see, for example, Ernest Gellhorn, "The Wages of Zealotry: The FTC under Seige," *Regulation Magazine* (January/February, 1980).

25. *Ibid.* Also see Muris, *supra* note 20.

26. Gellhorn, *supra* note 24, made this observation. Quote taken from Barry R. Weingast and Mark J. Moran, "The Myth of Runaway Bureaucracy: The Case of the FTC," *Regulation Magazine* (May/June, 1982). p. 35.

27. Jeffrey H. Joseph, Chamber of Commerce of the United States, Authorization Hearings, *supra* note 9, p. 69.

28. Elliot H. Levitas (D-Ga.), Authorization Hearings, *supra* note 9, p. 138.

29. Ernest Gellhorn and Glen Robinson, "Rulemaking 'Due Proc-

ess': An Inconclusive Dialogue," *The University of Chicago Law Review*, 48 (1981) p. 260.

30. Barry B. Boyer, Trade Regulation Rulemaking Procedures of the Federal Trade Commission: A Report to the Administrative Conference of the United States by the Special Project for the Study of Rulemaking Procedures Under the Magnuson-Moss Warranty-Federal Trade Commission Improvement Act (Report prepared for Congress by the Administrative Conference of the United States). Hereafter cited as Boyer Report, Phase I. Also, Boyer Report, Phase II, *supra* note 23.

31. Lon Fuller, "The Forms and Limits of Adjudication," *Harvard Law Review*, 91 (December, 1978) p. 366.

32. Boyer Report, Phase II, *supra* note 23, p. 16.

33. *Ibid.*, p. 43.

34. Muris, "Rules Without Reason," *supra* note 20, p. 24.

35. Henry B. Cabell, Report of the Presiding Officer on Proposed Trade Regulation Rule Regarding Advertising of Ophthalmic Goods and Services, 16 C.F.R. Part 456, Public Record 215–52, December 10, 1976.

36. Boyer Report, Phase II, *supra* note 23, Data Appendix, pp. 17–18.

37. Boyer Report, Phase I, *supra* note 30, Data Appendix, pp. 38–40; Boyer Report, Phase II, *supra* note 23, Data Appendix, p. 9.

38. In *American Optometric Association v. FTC*, *supra* note 21, the Second Circuit Court remanded portions of the Opthalmic TRR proscribing state bans on advertising largely because of a 1977 Supreme Court decision which it felt supplanted the need for the regulation and which raised new factual issues the Commission shoud consider. *Bates v. State Bar of Arizona*, 433 U.S. 350. At the same time, however, the Circuit Court emphasized the FTC's heightened obligation in justifying its rules under Magnuson-Moss requirements. As it stated at one point, for example, "there is almost no evidence, only speculation as to what have, since *Bates*, become the genuinely controversial aspects of the Commission's rule," p. 911.

39. *Katherine Gibbs School (Inc.) v. FTC*, *supra* note 21, pp. 663–64.

40. Boyer Report, Phases I and II, Data Appendices, *supra* notes 23, 30.

41. Boyer Report, Phase II, *supra* note 23, p. 54.

42. *Ibid.*, pp. 54–55.

43. *Katherine Gibbs School (Inc.) v. FTC*, *supra* note 21, pp. 665.

44. Boyer Report, Phase I, *supra* note 30, Data Appendix, pp. 38–40.

45. Boyer Report, Phase II, *supra* note 23, p. 76.

46. Boyer Report, Phase I, *supra* note 30, Data Appendix, pp. 89–90.

47. Author's interview, August, 1979.

48. Boyer Report, Phase II, *supra* note 310, pp. 18–19.

49. Stephen A. Nye and Eric M. Rabin, *FTC Rulemaking Procedures and Practice: Strategies for Private and Corporate Practitioners* (New York: Practicing Law Institute, 1977).

50. Author's interviews with presiding officers and other FTC officials, August, 1979.

51. *Washington Post* interview with Pertschuk, *supra* note 23.

52. Boyer, *supra* 3, p. 24.

53. Presiding Officer's Order No. 78: Certification to the Commission of Recommended Disputed Issues of Fact, August, 1979.

54. Author's interviews with presiding officers and other FTC officials, August, 1979.

55. For a general discussion of the limiting effects of due process requirements in this regard see Fuller, *supra* note 31.

56. Boyer Report, Phase I, *supra* note 30, Executive Summary, p. 32.

57. For a general discussion see Fuller, *supra* note 31.

58. *Home Box Office, Inc. v. FTC*, 567 F.2d 9 (D.C. Cir.), *cert. denied*, 434 U.S. 829 (1977).

59. Joseph, *supra* note 9, p. 69.

60. Jeremy Rabkin, "Rulemaking, Bias, and the Dues of Due Process at the FTC," *Regulation Magazine* (January/February, 1979) p. 45.

●7 Politics, Processes, and Administrative Policy Making

In the Introduction I argued that two basic perspectives should guide political scientists' analysis of administrative (and other) institutions. The causes and effects of formal structures and procedures can be partly understood within the context of group politics. That is, institutional choice frequently has important implications for competing interests who are affected by administration. In addition, however, administrative institutions reflect genuine normative concerns about bureaucracy and its proper role in the American political system, and can be explained and evaluated in part as efforts to promote desired values in agency decision making. The case of the FTC, as well as evidence cited in earlier chapters confirm the usefulness of both these perspectives in assessing recent developments in the process of regulatory administration.

THE DETERMINANTS AND SIGNIFICANCE OF PROCEDURAL CHOICE

Changes in the formal processes through which the FTC has sought to prevent unfair or deceptive practices have mirrored changes in other areas of regulatory administration over the past two decades. As discussed in Chapter 3, rulemaking has become much more prevalent as a means of carrying out statutory mandates. And as discussed in Chapter 4, Congress, the courts, and the executive have made increased efforts to guide and delimit rulemaking discretion through judicialized procedures, as well as through a variety of other devices. In these regards, the FTC's experience contributes to a more general understanding of the causes and effects of recent changes in the administrative process.

One is obliged to add, of course, that different regulatory agencies perform different missions within environments that vary along a number of dimensions. For instance, the breadth and the vagueness of the FTC's mandate may be unexceeded in the federal bureaucracy. Likewise, the Commission operates within a conflictual environment where regulated interests are generally opposed to government control. In contrast, some other agencies operate in more stable and harmonious environments, and their policies are generally perceived to benefit regulatees. These factors make the political content of FTC actions extreme, and as a result, they likely render the problems posed by the use of rulemaking and by judicialized rulemaking procedures especially acute. Notwithstanding such caveats, however, evidence suggests that the case of the FTC has important (if perhaps less dramatic) parallels.

Explaining Developments in the Administrative Process

Stephen Breyer and Richard Stewart hypothesize that the rulemaking revolution in regulatory administration has not been attributable so much to abstract considerations of formal justice as to bureaucratic self-interest. As demands for administrative action in response to new problems have outstripped administrative resources, they feel that rulemaking has become more and more attractive as an expedient way of achieving desired policy results.[1] Bruce Ackerman and William Hassler offer the complementary explanation that rulemaking has been encouraged or required by Congress and the courts in the interest of forceful and effective regulation. In this regard, Ackerman and Hassler speculate that the expanded use of rulemaking in the 1970s has resulted from the perception that the adjudicatory approach traditionally relied upon by administrators was an important element of the oft-criticized failure of agencies to regulate effectively. Thus, for example, many of the new agencies created since the mid–1960s have been required by their enabling statutes to issue rules.[2]

The FTC's experience is consistent with these explanations. By the early 1960s the Commission had become increasingly frustrated with adjudication because of its narrow substantive focus and because it could only be used to attack one industry member at a time. Likewise, Guides and Trade Practice Rules had proved to be of limited value because, as interpretive rules, they had no legal force. Rulemaking was adopted and later emphasized in part, therefore, because it was perceived by the agency as an effective way to satisfy growing demands for consumer-protection policy. At the same time, rulemaking was strongly encouraged by Congress, consumer advocates, and other observers of the FTC as a more forceful means of regulation. This was especially the case in the late 1960s and early 1970s as criticism of the Commission's alleged passiveness reached its high water mark.

The FTC's experience also helps explain the popularity of judicialized rulemaking procedures in recent years. In part, Magnuson-Moss requirements were a concession to industry groups who opposed strong consumer-protection policies. If the Commission was to have rulemaking authority, the business community sought to mitigate the impact of such a potentially powerful regulatory tool by securing procedures that would enable regulatees to challenge, delay, and discourage agency actions. Although no one has dealt with the topic in much detail, there is at least some evidence suggesting that due process requirements have been inspired by political considerations in other cases as well. For instance, in his 1972 study of formal and hybrid rulemaking procedures in several agencies, Robert Hamilton mentions that such requirements have typically been added at the behest of powerful industry groups. As the following passage suggests, battles among competing interests similar to the one which helped shape Magnuson-Moss procedures may be common:

There are problems with notice-and-comment rulemaking, however, that may be traced to a recurring problem in the administrative process: the apparent insensitivity of agencies to communications addressed to them. A person adversely affected in some way by a proposed rule may find little solace in the opportunity to submit written comment.... On the other hand, agency personnel and others desiring a prompt implementation of a regulatory program usually have little sympathy with such concerns. They believe that the agency will be careful, fair, and thorough, and object to more formal procedures as unnecessary. They also suggest that formal procedures are proposed to create delay in rulemaking rather than to improve the end-product of the rulemaking process. Congress becomes the battleground for these opposing views when a new statute granting rulemaking authority is being considered. To a surprising extent, Congress has become sympathetic to the fears expressed by persons who may be subject to regulation under a broad grant of rulemaking authority.[3]

If Magnuson-Moss procedures were due in part to group pressures, they also reflected broader, systemic concerns. Even some pro-regulation members of the House and Senate commerce committees were ambivalent about a delegation of rulemaking authority to the FTC. They felt that it was needed in the interest of effective consumer protection on the one hand, but on the other hand they were genuinely apprehensive about giving such broad legislative powers to unelected officials. As a response to this dilemma, due process requirements were added to ensure that TRRs were well reasoned *and* that affected interests would have ample opportunities to participate in and influence agency decision making. Relatedly, Magnuson-Moss procedures were designed to facilitate judicial review of FTC rules.

As discussed in Chapter 4, court decisions and statutes which have imposed judicialized rulemaking procedures on other agencies in recent years have reflected these same general goals. Moreover, other important efforts to structure agency discretion have also been intended to promote accountability, to facilitate public participation, and to ensure reasoned decisions. The greatly increased use of the legislative veto in the 1970s and the regulatory review programs of the Nixon, Ford, Carter, and Reagan administrations demonstrate a heightened desire for bureaucratic accountability. Likewise, the expansion of standing by the courts and the proliferation of various statutory provisions guaranteeing participation in the administrative process have been designed to ensure that agency decision makers are exposed to and take into account the viewpoints of relevant social interests. Finally, the increased use of cost-benefit analysis and related analytical techniques have been intended to encourage or guarantee well-reasoned and rigorously substantiated agency decisions.

The Consequences of Rulemaking and Rulemaking Procedure

While FTC rulemaking has undoubtedly been advantageous from a purely administrative standpoint, enabling the agency to formulate broad policies much more quickly that it could have through adjudication, it has also proved to be problematic from a political perspective. As a more forceful and precipitous means of implementing the Commission's mandate, rulemaking has contributed to the agency's unprecedented difficulties with Congress and other members of its environment in recent years.

Reliance on rulemaking, has had similar, if less dramatic, adverse political consequences in other regulatory areas. As discussed in Chapter 3, both William Cary and Skelly Wright explain the past reluctance of administrators to issue rules in these terms, citing anecdotes from a number of agencies in which occasional reliance on rulemaking had spurred especially strong opposition from regulated interests and rebuke from Congress.[4] More recently, Antonin Scalia has suggested that the rulemaking revolution throughout the federal bureaucracy has led to more "expansive interpretations of agency commands," and that this, in turn, is partially responsible for the widespread and intense reaction against regulation (and regulatory agencies) of the late 1970s and early 1980s.[5]

The effects of Magnuson-Moss procedures on FTC rulemaking also have broader implications. Hamilton's case studies of hybrid or formal procedures in several agencies document well the extra burden of substantiation and the delay imposed by such requirements. Discussing the effects of due process constraints on Food and Drug Administration rulemaking, for instance, he observes that

> the sixteen formal hearings that were held during the last decade vary from unnecessarily drawn out proceedings to virtual disasters. In not one instance did the agency complete a rulemaking proceeding involving a hearing in less than two years, and in two instances more than ten years elapsed between the first proposal and the final order. The *average* time elapse was roughly four years.[6]

In fact, Hamilton notes that the agency resource costs associated with judicialized procedures were so great that they often served as a disincentive to issue rules or as a lever which industry used to secure concessions on proposed regulations. In this latter regard he notes that "the principal effect of imposing rulemaking on a record has often been the dilution of the regulatory process rather than the protection of persons from arbitrary action."[7]

Similarly, Hamilton, Kenneth Davis, Peter Schuck, and others have found judicialized procedures to be inappropriate for dealing with the sorts of broad factual issues and value judgments inherent in many regulatory mandates. Speaking from experience as a former EPA official, Schuck argues that

> the litigation model's emphasis on reasoned argumentation and logical deductions from first principles makes it inappropriate for resolving certain kinds of regulatory issues.... Such problems ordinarily involve multiple criteria, and can be solved only by applying a number of standards whose relative weightings and orderings are sufficiently indeterminate as to imply no particular solution. Such a problem ... requires the exercise of substantial discretion rather than the application of preexisting decision rules, and its solution will often require interaction between the decision maker and others—interaction that would be inconsistent with the traditional norms of litigation.[8]

As with the FTC, Hamilton's case studies further suggest that the inflexibility of due process requirements has ultimately been an important source of delay. The fact that many regulations have been based on values or controversial scientific assertions has led to seemingly interminable debate and monumental records, yet administrators have still been unable to prove that the premises of their rules are correct.[9]

THE PURSUIT OF RATIONALITY AND RESPONSIVENESS

Although the choice of processes and procedures may result from narrow group interests, it is almost always debated and justified in terms of widely accepted norms concerning the way agency decisions ought to be made. In closing, therefore, it is worthwhile to examine more explicitly the broad, systemic values which have provided the basis for developments in the process of regulatory administration over the past two decades. In large part, attempts to structure agency discretion can be explained as efforts to promote one or both of two fundamental values: rationality and responsiveness. These are both laudable objectives and have long histories as guiding principles for administration. Yet important problems can arise from attempts to institutionalize each. Moreover, rationality and responsiveness are based on contradictory assumptions concerning the nature of agency decision making. Because of this, the attempt to achieve each militates against the attainment of the other, and the attempt to achieve both can strain and impair the administrative process in important ways.

Rationality and Responsiveness as Administrative Values

Substantive rationality in decision making means different things to different people. At the least, it implies the selection of means or behavior appropriate for achieving desired ends. A more ambitious definition of rationality includes the notion of comprehensiveness: the consideration of all factors relevant to a decision and the comparison of all feasible courses of action. Common to all definitions however, is the predetermination of goals and the objective consideration of proposed actions in terms of those goals.[10] In contrast, responsiveness connotes sensitivity to relevant values or interests. Unlike rationality, under which goals are given, the concept of responsiveness is based on the assumption that the decisional process involves the definition of objectives. Rationality and responsiveness each have an impressive heritage. As Martin Shapiro, Herbert Kaufman, and others have noted, these two goals have probably served as at least implicit guides in our thinking about bureaucracy and its role in government from the time of our founding fathers, and one or the other has provided the very foundation for practically every significant theory or model of the administrative process.[11]

Rationality lies at the heart of what is frequently referred to as the traditional or classical model of administration, the basic assumptions of which provided a unifying link in thinking about bureaucracy and its role in government from the late 1800s well into the 1930s. The idea that politics and administration are conceptually distinct and practically separable activities may have originated in Woodrow Wilson's 1883 essay "The Study of Administration."[12] At any rate, this perspective was a central element of progressive political theory and was widely accepted by students of government by the early part of the twentieth century. Influential writers of the period such as Frank Goodnow and Luther Gulick conceived of administration as a value-free selection of means for achieving ends already established through the political (legislative) process. As such, it should be informed by scientifically derived principles of sound management, as well as by substantive expertise.[13] In a 1937 work regarded by many as representing the zenith of the classical school, Gulick stated that

administration has to do with getting things done; with the accomplishment of defined objectives.... In the science of administration ... the basic "good" is efficiency. The fundamental objective of the science of administration is the accomplishment of the work at hand with the least expenditure of manpower and materials.[14]

The view of administration as an instrumental process was also reflected in legal thinking. According to Richard Stewart, the traditional model of administrative law began to develop in the 1860s and came to dominate the discipline for nearly a century. Several principles provided the basis for what became a reasonably coherent theory of the administrative process. First, statutes should define clear goals. Given this, agency decision-making procedures should be structured in such a way as to promote the "accurate, impartial, and rational application of legislative directives to given cases or classes of cases." Finally, the administrative process should also be designed to facilitate judicial review, since courts bore ultimate responsibility for ensuring the procedural and substantive correctness of agency decision making.[15]

The popularity of the traditional model is easy to understand, since it neatly reconciles delegation of authority with the principle of representative democracy. So long as bureaucrats pursue objective goals in an impartial, rational manner, the administrative process merely serves as an efficient "transmission belt" (to use Stewart's phrase) in attaining the popular will as expressed through the legislature. Indeed, given the assumptions of the traditional model, the delegation of authority to bureaucratic experts may well serve the ends of democracy better than detailed legislation. This theme, which was especially popular among New Deal intellectuals, has often served to justify broad grants of authority.[16]

The traditional model remains an important strain in our thinking about administrative performance. By the mid–1930s, however, some political scientists had clearly come to realize that, for a number of reasons, statutes often left controversial issues unresolved and that administration therefore became a "continuation of the legislative process."[17] In the 1940s, scholars such as Herbert Simon and Paul Appleby issued persuasive theoretical attacks against the notion of a dichotomy between politics and administration."[18] Thus many came to view the consideration of competing values by bureaucrats as not only a practical reality, but an inevitability.

The legal community took somewhat longer explicitly to recognize administration as more than an instrumental process. Although early commentators such as Ernst Freund realized that statutes occasionally delegated discretion, indefinite mandates were viewed as illegitimate (or at least undesirable) and generally avoidable.[19] Eventually, however, many administrative law scholars and jurists became resigned to the fact that

Congress often could not or would not define detailed administrative objectives, essentially passing controverted issues down to bureaucrats. As Stewart notes, "The unraveling of the notion of an objective goal for administration is reflected in statements by judges and legal commentators that the 'public interest is a texture of multiple strands,' that it is 'not a monolith,' and 'involves a balance of many interests.' "[20]

Given the realization that the administrative process involves value judgments, it has been a short step to the argument that agency decisions should reflect the interplay of social interests. Thus, the desire for responsiveness has emerged to compete with rationality as a guiding principle for administration. For example, this has manifested itself in a concern by students of government and law with such topics as representative bureaucracy and citizen participation. Of course, responsiveness affords a less satisfactory reconciliation between bureaucratic discretion and representative democracy than does rationality under the traditional model. However, it has been endorsed as the next best thing to policy making by elected representatives, given the need for Congress to delegate authority.

Institutionalizing Rationality and Responsiveness

Given the very different assumptions which they embody, one might logically assume that the norms of rationality and responsiveness have not served contemporaneously either as bases for administrative theory or as foundations for administrative institutions. Indeed, several scholars have argued that there has been a continual tension between the two throughout our history, with one and then the other assuming dominant status.[21] Thus, for example, Jacksonian democracy, with its emphasis on popularly controlled and representative bureaucracy, was supplanted by the Progressive movement and its emphasis on neutral efficiency. Interestingly, however, there seems to be some disagreement as to which of these goals has become dominant of late. This is probably due to the fact that our political system has attempted to institutionalize both ra-.

tionality and responsiveness in agency decision making in recent years.

Some important developments in the administrative process have obviously been informed by a desire to ensure responsiveness to affected interests. Thus, Richard Stewart argues convincingly that the expansion of standing by the courts since the early 1960s has reflected an abandonment of the traditional model of administrative law in favor of the notion that agency decision making should involve the balancing of interests.[22] Likewise, David Vogel feels that efforts to expand participation in agency decision making can be viewed as an attempt to institutionalize "interest group pluralism" at the administrative level. Vogel includes statutory requirements as well as judicial precedent in his analysis.[23] As discussed in Chapter 4, the former are diverse in character and often provide opportunities for outside parties to intervene at various stages of an agency's policy-making process.

Judicialized rulemaking procedures have also been designed to promote responsiveness by ensuring the viability of participation. Again, a common theme in the legislative histories and judicial opinions accompanying these requirements has been that the APA's informal rulemaking provides no assurance that the views and arguments of affected interests will be registered. Hearings are optional under this format and, when used, are conducted in an informal, legislative manner. Opportunities for affected parties to challenge regulations are limited, since courts can only overturn decisions found to be "arbitrary and capricious." In contrast, judicialized procedures may afford interested parties opportunities to challenge agency premises through cross-examination and the submission of competing studies and testimony. Furthermore, agencies are compelled to respond adequately to such challenges under threat of judicial review based on the much stricter "substantial evidence" criterion.

If our political system has attempted to facilitate interest representation in the administrative process in important respects, however, it has also attempted to promote rationality. As Colin Diver notes, the emphasis of rulemaking in lieu of case-by-case adjudication in recent years has clearly been consistent with the rational model of policy making.[24] One reason for this is that rulemaking is a more effective way for agencies to carry out their mandates. It can be used to establish regulatory policies quickly in a single proceeding, whereas adjudication is typically a slow and incremental means of developing standards. In addition, rulemaking is a more comprehensive policy-making device. It allows agencies to plan—to pursue coherent agendas, developing programs which anticipate future problems. Relatedly, it allows agencies to weigh all the considerations relevant to a particular problem. In contrast, adjudicatory policy making is frequently constrained by the need to deal exclusively or at least predominantly with the immediate facts presented by the cases being considered.

The greatly expanded use of cost-benefit analysis and related analytical tools can also be viewed as an effort to promote rationality in agency decision making. While rulemaking *allows* comprehensive planning, cost-benefit analysis is intended to ensure or at least to encourage a rigorous consideration of all the probable positive and negative effects of proposed actions. As discussed in Chapter 4, it reflects an instrumental model of agency decision making, with economic efficiency or net welfare serving as the predefined goal. Furthermore, it is designed to utilize relevant scientific and technical knowledge as a basis for administrative decisions. In these regards, one might conceive of cost-benefit analysis as an effort to institutionalize the goal of scientifically efficient administration advocated by Wilson, Gulick, and other writers of the traditional school.[25]

Finally, judicialized rulemaking procedures have been intended to ensure rationality in agency decision making in addition to promoting responsiveness. Indeed, they might be viewed as an effort to impose Stewart's traditional model of administrative law. While cross-examination, rebuttal, and decision making on the record have been designed in part to enhance the effectiveness of participation, they have also been intended to ensure that the factual, logical, and legal premises linking proposed actions with legislative intent are sound. Relatedly, they have been intended to ensure that such premises are made explicit so that they may be reviewed by the courts.

An assumption underlying judicialized rulemaking procedures is that objective goals are clearly evident from statutes and, accordingly, that proposed actions may be judged in terms of their appropriateness as means.

An Incoherent Approach

The fact that recent efforts to structure discretion reflect the values of rationality and responsiveness is perhaps not surprising, for both these qualities seem eminently desirable. As Charles Lindblom notes, however, although we have always wanted government decisions to be "informed and well analyzed" and also "democratic and political," these goals "call for contradictory features in policy making."[26] The two obviously reflect very different assumptions concerning the criteria for, as well as the process of, administration. The desire for rationality is based on the premise that administration is or can be a technocratic pursuit of legislatively defined goals. In contrast, the norm of responsiveness rests on the assumption that policy objectives have not been defined.

What are the implications of our attempts simultaneously to attain rationality and responsiveness? The two goals may complement one another in some contexts. To the extent that administration involves instrumental considerations, opportunities to challenge factual, logical, and legal premises may lead to sounder decisions. This has certainly been the rationale behind judicialized rulemaking procedures, for instance. Rationality and responsiveness are incompatible in other ways, however, and the pursuit of each logically interferes with the attainment of the other.

Again, the norm of responsiveness flows from the realization that administration is more than a technocratic process—that agency mandates entail value judgments which should be informed by the consideration of relevant social interests. If administration is legislative in substance, then the administrative process should be legislative as well, serving to accommodate competing demands. As means of ensuring instrumental rationality, devices such as judicialized rulemaking procedures and cost-benefit analysis inhibit such accommodation.

Judicialized rulemaking procedures reflect the premise that decisions proceed from first principles. They assume that the law, as it exists, can be imposed logically on a particular set of factual circumstances to yield one correct decision. Although they permit and indeed enhance participation (at least for those who can afford the requisite data, expert opinion, and legal talent), input is limited to "proofs and reasoned arguments."[27] Values and preferences, *per se*, are not relevant considerations. Likewise, judicialized procedures fail to allow for adjustment among competing interests, since the decision maker "is constrained to treat facts as unequivocally true and legal rules as unequivocally applicable."[28]

Cost-benefit analysis imposes similar limitations on agency decision making. Its predefined goal is economic efficiency, and it rests on the axiom that the marketplace provides an objective measure of policy consequences, either directly or by analogy through "shadow prices." As with judicialized rulemaking procedures, participation by interested parties is common under cost-benefit analysis. However, input is limited to the presentation of competing or supporting analyses (again, for those who can afford to prepare them); the direct confrontation of interests and bargaining are not legitimate considerations. As a leading student and former practitioner of cost-benefit analysis states, it is an inappropriate format for "the kind of balancing that goes on in the political process—people arguing and making their deals and whatever."[29]

Just as institutional mechanisms designed to promote instrumentally sound administration inhibit responsiveness, the expansion of opportunities to influence agency decision making is antithetical to rationality. This is obvious, since substantive rationality presumes objectivity and unity of purpose. The political science literature is replete with studies which attribute failure to achieve statutory goals during implementation to fragmented authority. As Paul Sabatier and Daniel Mazmanian state:

Numerous studies of the implementation of regulatory and social service programs have demonstrated that one of the principle obstacles is the difficulty of obtaining coordinated action within any agency and

among numerous semi-autonomous agencies involved in most implementation efforts.... Thus, one of the most important attributes of
any statute is the extent to which it hierarhically integrates the implementing agencies.[30]

Similarly, the provision of formal opportunities for outside
actors to influence the administrative process impairs the ability
of agencies to plan and to organize their internal resources in
a purposive way. As discussed in Chapter 4, for example, the
Consumer Products Safety Act originally provided such extensive opportunities to participate in the Consumer Products
Safety Commission's rulemaking that the agency finally persuaded Congress to delete or modify portions of the statute
allowing outside parties to initiate proceedings and formulate
policies. Under these petition and offerer requirements, the
Commission had been forced to spend a major share of its staff
man-hours analyzing and responding to outside grievances and
proposed standards. As a result, the agency found itself unable
to develop and pursue a coherent policy agenda.[31]

Implications for the Administrative Process

It bears emphasis that many regulatory agencies have been
affected by most or all of the developments discussed here.
Thus, opportunities to participate in and influence administrative decision making have been expanded, while at the same
time agencies have been encouraged or required to formulate
more comprehensive policies through institutions which require rational means-ends justifications. This has imposed considerable tension on the administrative process.

As Lindblom, Aaron Wildvasky, and others have argued,
comprehensive rationality, by itself, is extremely difficult or
impossible to attain in most policy-making contexts.[32] One reason for this is that the analytical burden implied by such an
approach is often staggering due to the complexity of the problems in question and to the likelihood that proposed alternative
solutions will have numerous direct and indirect consequences
for society (many of which are interrelated). Because difficulties of this sort pose such a formidable obstacle to comprehen-

sive means-ends analysis, decision makers often adopt a more manageable, incremental approach, dealing with smaller elements of larger problems on a piecemeal basis. Given the infeasibility of comprehensive analysis, an advantage of incremental decision making is that mistakes will be small and easy to correct.

Another problem with the rational model is that it presumes that values or objectives are clearly defined at the outset of the decision-making process and that they will subsequently serve as guides for the analysis of policy alternatives. In practice, however, this is often not the case. Many policy alternatives have differential effects with regard to two or more competing values, and it is unrealistic to assume that individual decision makers have neatly ranked and assigned weights to their preferences. Even more important, policy decisions in a democracy must often reflect the different value structures of different individuals. In light of these realities, the definition of objectives and the consideration of policy alternatives typically occur simultaneously rather than sequentially. Further, the test of good or acceptable policy is that which is agreed upon, perhaps for different reasons by different people. Such agreement is not based on objective analysis (at least wholly), but instead is arrived at through political modes of conflict resolution.

An important implication of institutional developments in the administrative process designed to promote comprehensive rationality is that they have militated against the use of non-rational decision-making techniques. Obviously, increased reliance on rulemaking in lieu of case-by-case adjudication has been a more comprehensive (as opposed to incremental) strategy for implementing statutory mandates. While there is much to be said for such an approach—at least in theory—the emphasis of rulemaking has also meant that agencies have had to deal with large and more complex policy issues at once. This, in turn, has increased the analytical burdens associated with individual administrative actions. It has also increased both the probability and the potential ill effects of miscalculations.

Likewise, procedures designed to ensure that agency decisions are instrumentally sound have discouraged the use of non-rational techniques for reconciling competing values. Cost-benefit analysis and judicialized procedures are based at least implicitly on the assumption that policy objectives are evident from statutory commands. In practice, however, this is frequently not the case. Although the FTC Act is perhaps an extreme example of a politically laden mandate, there are certainly numerous other regulatory statutes which fail to resolve conflict among competing interests. Furthermore, the emphasis of rulemaking as a means of implementing these mandates in recent years has added to the political content of individual decisions by increasing the number and often the diversity and intensity of affected interests.

If requirements designed to promote comprehensive rationality in the administrative process have often been inappropriate given the nature of the issues agencies must deal with, institutions intended to ensure responsiveness have exacerbated the problem. The expansion of interest representation has made the milieu of agency decision making more complex or polycentric as the number of actors and issues to be considered has increased. As Stewart asserts, it has created an "unruly field of shifting forces that may defy regular ordering."[33] Thus, the decisional burden confronting administrators has become more legislative because of developments such as the expansion of standing and the statutory provision of opportunities for outside individuals, groups, and institutions to intervene in agency decision making. At the same time, however, agency officials have been rendered less able to rely on legislative modes of problem solving and conflict resolution.

The strain generated by recent institutional developments has aggravated traditional problems of regulatory administration. Delay (or deadlock) and high resource costs are natural accompaniments to institutions which require agencies to provide rational justifications for policies, and which also afford interested parties substantial opportunities to intervene and to challenge proposed actions. A fundamental reason for this is that the data, expert opinions, and legal arguments relevant to a decision will seldom all point in the same direction. This is especially true where regulations are issued pursuant to vague mandates and have wide-ranging social, economic, medical, environmental, or other effects. Delay may result from protracted court battles over the rightness or wrongness of agency policies, or may occur beforehand as administrators struggle assiduously to develop tight cases.

Delay has often been extreme under due process requirements, as discussed. It has been attributable in part to time spent in hearings accommodating the rights of participants to testify, cross-examine, and rebut. A related but more important source of delay under judicialized rulemaking procedures has been the analytical burden placed upon administrators by outside parties. Agencies have often spent years developing legal theories, collecting data, and preparing analyses which will withstand the competing efforts of rule opponents and, ultimately, judicial review.

Interest group representation within the context of cost-benefit analysis and related decisional constraints can produce similar results. For example, groups have sometimes used their ability to challenge environmental impact statements to produce "analysis paralysis."[34] It should also be noted that the effects of these devices and judicialized rulemaking procedures may reinforce one another. Where both obtain, an agency's estimation of costs and benefits may be subject to challenge in adversarial proceedings and may constitute part of the record upon which it must base its final decision.

Efforts to institutionalize rationality and responsiveness can have other undesirable effects as well. Since rationality requirements preclude the expression of "naked interests," values and preferences must be disguised in the form of competing studies, expert testimony, legal arguments, and the like. Participants in numerous regulatory proceedings have manipulated parameters such as discount rates to produce self-serving cost-benefit analyses, for example.[35] This mode of policy advocacy presents several problems.

One is that it is expensive and therefore biased in favor of well-financed groups. If the ability to marshal data and reasoned arguments to support one's interests has always been a source of unequal advantage in the administrative process, recent developments have certainly intensified the problem. Available evidence suggests that a competent cost-benefit analysis may often require several hundred thousand dollars,[36] and that the data and legal talent needed for effective participation in judicialized rulemaking proceedings can entail similar expenditures.[37] Some groups are obviously much better able to compete under these constraints than others.

Another problem is that democratic accountability suffers to the extent that interests are expressed as technical or legal arguments which only specialists can comprehend. In a related sense, the integrity of administration is undermined if processes of accommodation must take place behind the scenes in violation of the purpose of an agency's prescribed decision-making procedures. But again, the expansion of interest representation has increased the need for accommodation under broad regulatory mandates by affording substantial opportunities for outside parties to obstruct agency action.

CONCLUSION

The dramatic expansion of delegated authority in recent years has been accompanied by a proliferation of requirements intended to structure the exercise of bureaucratic discretion. There are two general explanations for this trend. First, administrative policy making has naturally become more and more significant to a wider range of affected interests. In turn, groups have increasingly come to appreciate the fact that the rules of the game can have important substantive implications and, as a result, have frequently sought formal institutions which would later give them strategic advantages in their efforts to influence agency decision making.

A second explanation for the increased popularity of structural devices is that we have simply developed strong misgivings about the continued delegation of policy-making authority. Founded on basic constitutional principles concerning proper institutional roles, these misgivings have been reinforced by growing doubts about the quality of unconstrained bureaucratic discretion. The expertise and professionalism of administrators were once assumed to promote efficient, rational decisions.[38] Likewise, administrators were once assumed to be responsive to affected interests.[39] In recent years, however, agency officials have come under attack for their parochial views which allegedly cause them to pursue narrow programs at the expense of the broader public interest. Charges of agency capture and quiescence have also eroded confidence that administrators are either neutral or evenly representative in their orientation. In light of these doubts, we have structured the administrative process in order to make agencies more accountable and to promote desired qualities in their decision making.

The emphasis on structural constraints in regulatory administration has clearly increased the relevance of institutional policy analysis for students of public administration. Such analysis is nowhere more appropriate, moreover, than in the area of rulemaking, which is the most visible and direct means by which agencies make policy. The generalizations offered here concerning the use of rulemaking and efforts to structure rulemaking discretion should obviously be regarded as tentative ones given the limited scope of the study. At the very least, however, the case of the FTC and evidence from other agencies demonstrate that choices among formal processes and procedures can pose highly salient political issues and can ultimately have important policy effects, both intended and unintended. This is not to say, of course, that policy analysis should dwell on formal institutions to the exclusion of other factors. Rather, rules and structures can be usefully integrated with other considerations, such as environmental pressures and the perspectives of agency personnel, to yield a more complete understanding of the administrative policy-making process.

NOTES

1. Stephen G. Breyer and Richard B. Stewart, *Administrative Law and Regulatory Policy* (Boston: Little, Brown, and Company, 1979) pp. 403–4.

2. Bruce Ackerman and William Hassler, "Beyond the New Deal: Coal and the Clean Air Act," *Yale Law Journal*, 89 (1980) p. 1474.

3. Robert W. Hamilton, "Procedures for the Adoption of Rules of General Applicability: The Need for Procedural Innovation in Administrative Rulemaking," *California Law Review*, 60 (1972) p. 1314.

4. William L. Cary, *Politics and the Regulatory Agencies* (New

York: McGraw-Hill Book Company, 1967); J. Skelly Wright, "Beyond Discretionary Justice," *Yale Law Journal,* 81 (1972).

5. Antonin Scalia, "Back to Basics: Making Law Without Rules," *Regulation Magazine* (July/August, 1981) p. 26.

6. Hamilton, *supra* note 3, p. 1287.

7. *Ibid.,* pp. 1312–13.

8. Peter Schuck, "Litigation, Bargaining, and Regulation," *Regulation Magazine* (July/August, 1979) pp. 28–29.

9. Hamilton, *supra* note 3.

10. Numerous writers have discussed rationality in decision making. See, for example, Herbert A. Simon, *Administrative Behavior* (New York: The Free Press, 1947); David Braybrooke and Charles E. Lindblom, *A Strategy of Decision* (London: The Free Press of Glencoe, 1963).

11. Herbert Kaufman, "Emerging Conflicts in the Doctrines of Public Administration," *American Political Science Review,* 50 (December, 1956); Kaufman, "Administrative Decentralization and Political Power," *Public Administration Review,* 29 (January/February, 1969); Martin Shapiro, "On Predicting the Future of Administrative Law," *Regulation Magazine* (May/June, 1982).

12. Woodrow Wilson, "The Study of Administration," *Political Science Quarterly,* 2 (June, 1887).

13. Frank Goodnow, *Politics and Administration,* (New York: Putnam, 1900); Luther L. Gulick and L. Urwick, eds. *Papers in the Science of Administration* (New York: Institute of Public Administration, 1937).

14. Gluick, "Science, Values, and Administration," in Gulick and Urwick, eds., *supra* note 13, p. 192.

15. Richard B. Stewart, "The Reformation of American Administrative Law," *Harvard Law Review,* 88 (1975) pp. 1672–75.

16. See, for example, James M. Landis, *The Administrative Process* (New Haven: Yale University Press, 1938); Louis Brownlow, ed., *Report of the President's Committee on Administrative Management* (Washington, D.C.: U.S. Government Printing Office, 1937).

17. Pendleton Herring, *Public Administration and the Public Interest* (New York: McGraw-Hill Book Company, 1936) p. 218.

18. Simon, *supra* note 10; Paul H. Appleby, *Policy and Administration* (University, Alabama: University of Alabama Press, 1949).

19. Ernst Freund, *Administrative Powers Over Persons and Property* (Chicago: University of Chicago Press, 1928) pp. 71–103.

20. Stewart, *supra* note 15, p. 1683.

21. See, for example, Kaufman and Shapiro, *supra* note 11.

22. Stewart, *supra* note 15.

23. David Vogel, "The Public Interest Movement and the American Reform Tradition," *Political Science Quarterly*, 95 (Winter, 1981).

24. Colin S. Diver, "Policymaking Paradigms in Administrative Law," *Harvard Law Review*, 95 (1981).

25. For an elaboration of this argument see Frederick C. Thayer, "Prodictivity: Taylorism Revisited (Round Three)," *Public Administration Review*, 32 (November/December, 1972).

26. Charles E. Lindblom, *The Policy-Making Process* (Englewood Cliffs, New Jersey: Prentice-Hall, 1980) p. 12.

27. Lon Fuller, "The Forms and Limits of Adjudication," *Harvard Law Review*, 91 (December, 1978).

28. Schuck, *supra* note 8, p. 28.

29. Statement of Bernard Fischoff, "The Use of Cost-Benefit Analysis by Regulatory Agencies," Joint Hearings Before the Subcommittee on Oversight and Investigations and the Subcommittee on Consumer Protection and Finance of the Committee on Interstate and Foreign Commerce of the U. S. House of Representatives, 96th Cong., 1st Sess., p. 25.

30. Paul A. Sabatier and Daniel A. Mazmanian, "The Implementation of Public Policy: A Framework of Analysis," *Policy Studies Journal*, special issue (1980) p. 546.

31. Author's conversation with members of the Consumer Product Safety Commission General Counsel's Office, February, 1983.

32. Braybrooke and Lindblom, *supra* note 10; Lindblom, "The Science of Muddling Through," *Public Administration Review* (Spring, 1959); and Aaron Wildvasky, *The Politics of the Budgetary Process*, 2d. ed. (Boston: Little, Brown, and Company, 1974).

33. Stewart, *supra* note 15, p. 1779.

34. Lester C. Thurow, *The Zero-Sum Society* (New York: Basic Books, 1980); Eugene Bardach and Lucian Pugliaresi, "The Environmental Impact Statement vs. The Real World," *The Public Interest*, 49, (Fall, 1977).

35. Julius Allen, *Costs and Benefits of Federal Regulations: An Overview*. Congressional Research Service Report No. 78–152 E., 1978.; Michael S. Baram, "Cost-Benefit Analysis: An Inadequate Basis for Health, Safety, and Environmental Regulatory Decisionmaking," *Ecology Law Quarterly*, 8 (1980).

36. Milton J. Socolar, acting comptroller general of the United States, GAO Report to the Committee on Governmental Affairs of the U. S. Senate. Delivered June 23, 1981.

37. Roger C. Crampton, "The Why, Where, and How of Broadened Public Participation in the Administrative Process," *Georgetown Law Review*, 60 (1972).

38. This is evident from such influential works of the 1930s as James Landis' *The Administrative Process* and the Brownlow Commission's report, for example. *Supra* note 16.

39. See, for example, Norton E. Long, "Bureaucracy and Constitutionalism," *American Political Science Review*, 46 (September, 1952).

• Bibliography

Ackerman, Bruce, and William Hassler. "Beyond the New Deal: Coal and the Clean Air Act." *Yale Law Journal*, 89 (1980), 1466–1556.

Allen, Carleton K. *Bureaucracy Triumphant*. London: Oxford University Press, 1931.

Anderson, James. *Public Policy-Making*. New York: Praeger Publishers, 1975.

Appleby, Paul H. *Policy and Administration*. University, Alabama: University of Alabama Press, 1949.

Baker, Warren E. "Policy by Rule or Ad Hoc Approach—Which Should It Be?" *Law and Contemporary Problems*, 22 (1957), 658–71.

Baram, Michael S. "Cost-Benefit Analysis: An Inadequate Basis for Health, Safety and Environmental Regulatory Decisionmaking." *Ecology Law Quarterly*, 8 (1980), 473–531.

Barber, Sotrios A. *The Constitution and the Delegation of Congressional Power*. Chicago: University of Chicago Press, 1975.

Bardach, Euguen, and Lucian Pugliaresi. "The Environmental Impact Statement vs. The Real World." *The Public Interest*, 49 (Fall, 1977), 22–38.

Beck, James M. *Our Wonderland of Bureaucracy*. New York: Macmillan Publishing Company, 1932.

Bernstein, Marver. *Regulating Business by Independent Commission* Princeton, New Jersey: Princeton University Press, 1955.

Bonfield, Arthur. "Representing the Poor in Federal Rulemaking." *Michigan Law Review*, 67 (1969), 511.

Bonfield, Arthur. "Public Participation in Federal Rulemaking Re-

lating to Public Property, Loans, Grants, Benefits or Contracts."
University of Pennsylvania Law Review, 119 (1970).

Boyer, Barry B. "Trade Regulation Rulemaking Procedures of the Federal Trade Commission: A Report to the Administrative Conference of the United States by the Special Project for the Study of Rulemaking Procedures Under the Magnuson-Moss Warranties-Federal Trade Commission Improvement Act. "Report presented to Congress by the Administrative Conference of the United States, Washington, D.C., 1979.

Boyer, Barry B. "Too Many Lawyers, Not Enough Practical People." *Law and Policy Quarterly*, 5 (January, 1983).

Braybrooke, David, and Charles E. Lindblom. *A Strategy of Decision.* London: The Free Press of Glencoe, 1963.

Breyer, Stephen G., and Richard B. Stewart. *Administrative Law and Regulatory Policy.* Boston: Little, Brown and Company, 1979.

Brownlow, Louis, ed. *Report of the President's Committee on Administrative Management.* Washington, D.C.: U.S. Government Printing Office, 1937.

Cary, William L. *Politics and the Regulatory Agencies.* New York: McGraw-Hill Book Company, 1967.

Checkoway, Barry, and Jon Van. "What Do We Know About Citizen Participation? A Selective Review of Research." In *Citizen Participation in America.* Ed. Stuart Langton. Lexington, Massachusetts: Lexington Books, 1978.

Comer, John P. *Legislative Functions of National Adminsitrative Authorities.* New York: Columbia University Press, 1927.

Crampton, Roger C. "The Why, Where, and How of Broadened Public Participation in Administrative Process." *Georgetown Law Review*, 60 (1972), 525.

Creighton, Lucy Black. *Pretenders to the Throne.* Lexington, Massachusetts: Lexington Books, 1976.

Cushman, Robert E. "The Constitutional Status of Independent Regulatory Commissions." *Cornell Law Quarterly*, 24 (1938) 163–97.

Davis, Kenneth Culp. *Administrative Law and Government.* St. Paul, Minnesota: West Publishing Company, 1975.

Davis, Kenneth Culp. *Discretionary Justice.* Baton Rouge, Louisiana: Louisiana State University Press, 1969.

Davis, Kenneth Culp. *Administrative Law Government.* St. Paul, Minnesota: West Publishing Company, 1975.

Diver, Colin S. "Policymaking Paradigms in Administrative Law." *Harvard Law Review*, 95 (December, 1981), 393–434.

Edelman, Murray. "Symbols and Political Quiescence." *American Political Science Review*, 54 (September, 1960), 695–704.

Ellis, Dorsey D., Jr. "Legislative Powers: FTC Rulemaking." In *The Federal Trade Commission Since 1970: Economic Regulation and Bureaucratic Behavior.* Eds. Kenneth Clarkson and Timothy J. Muris. Cambridge, Massachusetts: Cambridge University Press, 1981.

Elman, Philip. "Rulemaking Procedure in the FTC's Enforcement of the Merger Law." *Harvard Law Review*, 78 (1964), 385–391.

Elman, Philip. "Administrative Reform in the Federal Trade Commission." *The Georgetown Law Journal*, 59 (1971).

Fiorina, Morris. *Congress: Keystone of Washington Establishment.* New Haven: Yale University Press, 1977.

Freedman, James O. *Crisis and Legitimacy: The Administrative Process and American Government.* Cambridge: Cambridge University Press, 1978.

Freund, Ernst. *Administrative Powers Over Persons and Property.* Chicago: University of Chicago Press, 1978.

Fritschler, A. Lee. *Smoking and Politics.* Englewood Cliffs, New Jersey: Prentice-Hall, 1969.

"FTC Substantive Rulemaking: An Evaluation of Past Practice and Proposed Legislation." *New York University Law Review*, 48 (1973), 135–70.

Fuller, Lon. "The Forms and Limits of Adjudication." *Harvard Law Review*, 91 (December, 1978), 353–409.

Gellhorn, Ernest. "The FTC Under Seige." *Regulation Magazine* (January/February, 1980), 33–40.

Gellhorn, Ernest, and Glen Robinson. "Rulemaking 'Due Process' An Inconclusive Dialogue." *The University of Chicago Law Review*, 48 (1981), 201–62.

Gillespie, Judith A., and Dina A. Zinnes, eds. *Missing Elements in Political Inquiry.* Beverly Hills: Sage Publications, 1982.

Gulick, Luther L., and L. Urwick, eds. *Papers in the Science of Administration.* New York: Institute of Public Administration, 1937.

Hamilton, Robert W. "Procedures for the Adoption of Rules and of General Applicability: The Need for Procedural Innovation in Administrative Rulemaking." *California Law Review*, 60 (1972), 1276–1337.

Hart, James. *The Ordinance Making Power of the President of the United States.* Baltimore: The Johns Hopkins Press, 1925.

Hart, James. "The Exercise of Rulemaking Power." *Report of the President's Committee on Administrative Management.* Washington, D.C.: U.S. Government Printing Office, 1937.

Herring, Pendleton. *Public Administration and the Public Interest.* New York: McGraw-Hill Book Company, 1936.

Hewart, Gordon. *The New Despotism.* London: Ernest Benn, 1929.

Jones, Charles O. *An Introduction to the Study of Public Policy.* North Scituate, Massachusetts: Duxbury Press, 1977.

Jowell, Jeffery L. *Law and Bureaucracy: Administrative Discretion and the Limits of Legal Action.* Port Washington, New York: Dunellen Publishing Company, 1975.

Kaufman, Herbert. "Emerging Conflicts in the Doctrines of Public Administration." *American Political Science Review,* 50 (December, 1956), 1057–73.

Kaufman, Herbert. "Administrative Decentralization and Political Power." *Public Administration Review,* 29 (January/February, 1969), 3–15.

Landis, James M. *The Administrative Process.* New Haven: Yale University Press, 1938.

Laski, Harold. "The Limitations of the Expert." *Harper's Monthly Magazine,* 101 (1930).

Lindblom, Charles E. "The Science of Muddling Through." *Public Administration Review,* 19 (Spring, 1959), 79–88.

Lindblom, Charles E. *The Policy Making Process.* Englewood Cliffs, New Jersey: Prentice-Hall, 1980.

Long, Norton E. "Bureaucracy and Constitutionalism." *American Political Science Review,* 46 (September 1952), 808–818.

Lowi, Theodore, J. *The End of Liberalism.* New York: W. W. Norton, 1979.

McConnell, Grant. *Private Power and American Democracy.* New York: Alfred A. Knopf, 1966.

McFarland, James. "Landis' Report: The Voice of One Crying Out in the Wilderness." *Virginia Law Review,* 47 (1961), 373–438.

Mayhew, David. *Congress: The Electoral Connection.* New Haven: Yale University Press, 1974.

Mayton, William. "The Legislative Resolution of the Rulemaking Versus Adjudication Problem in Agency Lawmaking." *Duke Law Journal* (1980), 103–135.

Muris, Timothy J. "Rules Without Reason: The Case of the FTC." *Regulation Magazine,* (September/October, 1982), 20–26.

Nichols, Albert L., and Richard Zeckhauser. "Government Comes to the Workplace: An Assessment of OSHA." *The Public Interest,* 49 (Fall, 1977), 39–69.

Norton, Clark F. *Congressional Review, Deferral, and Dissapproval of Executive Actions: A Summary and an Inventory of Statutory*

Authority. Rpt. 76–88G. Washington, D.C.: Congressional Research Service, 1976.

Nye, Stephen A., and Eric M. Rabin. *FTC Rulemaking Procedures and Practice: Strategies for Private and Corporate Practitioners.* New York: Practicing Law Institute, 1977.

Ostrom, Vincent. "A Forgotten Tradition: The Constitutional Level of Analysis" In *Missing Elements in Political Inquiry.* Eds. Judith A. Gillespie and Dina A. Zinnes. Beverly Hills: Sage Publications, 1982.

Peck, Cornelius. "The Atrophied Rulemaking Powers of the National labor Relations Baord." *Yale Law Journal,* 70 (1967), 729–61.

Pederson, William. "Formal Records and Informal Rulemaking." *Yale Law Journal,* 85 (1975), 38–88.

Peters, Guy. *The Politics of Bureaucracy: A Comparative Perspective.* New York: Longmans, 1978.

Sabatier, Paul A., and Daniel A. Mazmanian. "The Implementation of Public Policy: A Framework of Analysis," *Policy Studies Journal* (special issue, 1980), 538–60.

Sabatier, Paul A., and Daniel A. Mazmanian. *The Implementation of Public Policy.* Glenview, Illinois: Scott, Foresman, and Company, 1983.

Scalia, Antonin. "Back to Basics: Making Law Without Rules." *Regulation Magazine* (July/August, 1981), 25–28.

Schuck, Peter. "Litigation, Bargaining, and Regulation." *Regulation Magazine* (July/August, 1979), 26–34.

Shapiro, David L. "The Choice of Rulemaking or Adjudication in the Development of Administrative Policy." *Harvard Law Review,* 78 (1965), 921–72.

Shapiro, Martin. "On Predicting the Future of Administrative Law." *Regulation Magazine* (May/June, 1982) 18–25.

Sherwood, Foster H. "The Federal Administrative Procedure Act." *American Political Science Review,* 41 (April, 1947), 271–293.

Simon, Herbert A. *Administrative Behavior.* New York: The Free Press, 1947.

Stein, Harold. "Public Agencies as Political Actors." In *Current Issues in Public Administration.* Ed. Frederick S. Lane. New York: St. Martin's Press, 1978.

Stewart, Richard B. "The Reformation of American Administrative Law." *Harvard Law Review,* 88 (June, 1975), 1669–1813.

Stokey, Edith, and Richard Zeckhauser. *A Primer for Policy Analysis.* New York: W. W. Norton, 1978.

Stone, Alan. *Economic Regulation and the Public Interest: The Federal*

Trade Commission in Theory and Practice. Ithaca, New York: Cornell University Press, 1977.

Thayer, Frederick C. "Productivity: Taylorism Revisited (Round Three)." Public Administration Review, 32 (November/December, 1972), 833–840.

Thompson, Frank J. "Bureaucratic Discretion and the National Health Service Corps." Political Science Quarterly, 97 (Fall, 1982), 427–445.

Thompson, Mark S. Benefit-Cost Analysis for Program Evaluation. Beverly Hills: Sage Publications, 1980.

Thurow, Lester C. The Zero-Sum Society. New York: Basic Books, 1980.

Verkuil, Paul R. "Jawboning Administrative Agencies: Ex Parte Contracts by the White House." Columbia Law Review, 80 (1980), 943–89.

Vogel, David. "The Public Interest Movement and the American Reform Tradition." Political Science Quarterly, 95 (Winter, 1981), 607–627.

Weidenbaum, Murray L. Business, Government and the Public. Englewood Cliffs, New Jersey: Prentice Hall, Inc., 1981.

Weingast, Barry R., and Mark J. Moran. "The Myth of Runaway Bureaucracy: The Case of the FTC." Regulation Magazine. (May/June, 1982), 33–38.

West, William F. "The Politics of Administrative Rulemaking," Public Administration Review, 42 (September/October, 1982), 420–426.

Weston Robert. "Deceptive Advertising and the FTC," The Federal Bar Journal, 24 (June, 1964).

Wildvasky, Aaron. The Politics of the Budgetary Process. Boston: Little, Brown and Company, 1974.

Wilson James Q. "The Dead Hand of Regulation." The Public Interest, 25 (1971), 45–61.

Wilson James Q. "The Rise of the Bureaucratic State." In Current Issue in Public Administration. Ed. Fedrick S. Lane New York: St. Martin's Press, 1978.

Wilson, Woodrow. "The Study of Administration." Political Science Quarterly, 2 (June, 1887), 197–222.

Wright, J. Skelly "Beyond Discretionary Justice." Yale Law Journal, 81 (January, 1982), 575–597.

• Index

ABOUT THE AUTHOR

WILLIAM F. WEST is Assistant Professor of Political Science at Texas A&M University. He has published articles in *Public Policy*, the *Public Administration Review*, and *Political Science Quarterly*.